THE BOOK OF SOBA

THE BOOK OF
SOBA

JAMES UDESKY

Foreword by *WILLIAM SHURTLEFF*

KODANSHA INTERNATIONAL
Tokyo • New York • London

To Grandmother Haus, whose strong constitution and love of nature nurtured me in my youth, and to my mother and father, whose continual patience and assistance allowed me to see this project through to completion.

Note: All recipes in this book use the American cup which equals 240 cc. Metric conversions have been provided for convenience.

Cooperation and invaluable assistance in the production of this book were given by the following soba shops, companies, and associations: Honjinbo, Take Yabu, Asanoya, Honmura-an. Kikkoman, Ozeki, Ishimori Seifun-jo, Odakyu Department Store (in Shinjuku), Seibu Department Store (in Ikebukuro), Matsuya Department Store (in Ginza), Nushisa Shikki-ten. Federation of Japan Noodle Organizations, Japan Buckwheat Millers Association.

CREDITS: Photography by Tamahisa Ejiri. Additional photographs: Tetsu Hayakawa, pp. 20, 22–42, 159; Federation of Japan Noodle Organizations, pp. 6, 19; *Ukiyo-e* and *Nihonga* prints courtesy of Jyutaro Yamamoto. Sketches in recipe sections by Reiko Michida. Sketch on page 145 by Ryosuke Kami.

Published by Kodansha International Ltd., 17–14 Otowa 1-chome, Bunkyo-ku, Tokyo 112, and Kodansha America, Inc.

Distributed in the United States by Kodansha America, Inc., 114 Fifth Avenue, New York, New York 10011, and in the United Kingdom and continental Europe by Kodansha Europe Ltd., 95 Aldwych, London WC2B 4JF.

Library of Congress Cataloging-in-Publication Data

Udesky, James.
The book of soba.
  Bibliography: p. 238. Includes index.
  1. Cookery (Buckwheat) 2. Soba (Noodles) 3. Cookery, Japanese. I. Title.
TX809.B8U28 1988 641.8'22 87–82855

ISBN 4-7700-1956-4

CONTENTS

Foreword

It is a great honor and pleasure for me to write the fore-word to *The Book of Soba*. Since my friend James Udesky outlined his long-term project to me some years ago, I have followed its progress with great interest. His efforts have borne fruit, and the result is an important and original contribution.

Although the Japanese word "soba" also refers to the buckwheat plant and its seeds, I will use it here to refer only to buckwheat noodles, which are one of Japan's most important traditional foods. Soba is a food both democratic and elite, distinguished by being indispensable in both Japan's popular food culture and in its classic haute cuisine. To understand soba is to understand the heart of Japanese food culture. Indeed the world of soba in Japan is a microcosm of the best of all Japanese culture.

My wife Akiko and I lived in Japan for seven years (1971–77) studying foods, and especially soy foods such as tofu, miso, soy sauce, and *natto*. For us the word "soba" brings back a host of good memories. Many a time at Kyoto's Izumo Soba we used to watch the crafts-man make handmade soba in the shop's front window. He would roll out the dough into a huge thin round using a slender yard-long wooden rolling pin, then fold it serpentine-fashion, and deftly slice it crosswise with an elegant five-inch-tall soba knife into tender, fresh noodles. Here, I thought, was the Japanese counterpart of Italy's tosser of fresh pizza rounds.

My favorite at Izumo was Soba Noodles with Whipped Mountain Yam, the freshly grated yam atop the soba in a steaming hot broth. This type of hot soba was exquisite on cold winter nights! In inexpensive but cozy restaurants we enjoyed noodles and tempura served on a graceful little tray of thin bamboo strips and accompanied by a separate cup of dipping sauce. I still have visions of the young man from the local soba shop racing on his bicycle with an order for home delivery balanced skillfully on one hand above his head. Twice we traveled to the Nagano-Shinshu area, the center of buckwheat growing and processing in Japan. And each New Year's Eve, like all Japanese, we downed *Toshikoshi Soba*, which carries its own wish for a long life in the new year and years ahead.

To enjoy and study soba at its elegant best, we visited Yabu Soba in Kanda, Tokyo. We immediately sensed that this famous generations-old soba shop was special—the home of an almost timeless, pure Japanese form: the elegant yet simple decor, the beautiful utensils and fabrics, the presence of nature, the warm and attentive service, and the satisfying light food.

We are not the first generation of Westerners to take a deep interest in Japanese foods. The first were those European travelers who managed to enter isolated Japan during the 1600s and 1700s. From men like Captain John Saris (1613), Englebert Kaempfer (1712), Per Osbeck (1771), and Karl Peter Thunberg (1784), we get our first sketches of a world of food and drink vastly different from our own. Kaempfer traveled in Japan from 1690 to 1692. In his classic *Amoenitatum Exoticarum*, published in Latin in Germany in 1712, he gave the Chinese character for buckwheat, then wrote, "Kjo [pronounced Kyo], vulgo Soba, Fagopyrum sativum. Frumentum Sarasenicum." He made no mention of buckwheat noodles.

The second wave arrived in the 1880s, after Commodore Matthew Perry had forced Japan to open its doors to Western influence. The emperor Meiji imported a host of top European professors to staff his new universities, and many of those wrote extensively about Japanese foods, often in great detail.

The third wave of interest arose some ninety years later, following World War II, and many of these traveler-students had their roots in the American and European natural-food and macrobiotic movements. Many learned Japanese, focused on the study of a small group of important foods, and wrote. Equally important, they generally worked to export to their native countries the foods they were studying. By the late 1970s large amounts of traditional Japanese foods were already being imported to the Western world and enjoyed by a new health-conscious generation.

Akiko and I are part of this most recent wave, as is James Udesky. We first had the pleasure of meeting James in January 1976 in San Francisco. He was studying with Noboru Muramoto, a Japanese teacher of macrobiotics, and was deeply interested in *mochi*, herbs, and miso. We met again in Japan later that year— James had come to buy *mochi* machines. I encouraged him to pursue his interest in studying Japanese foods and shared with him some of my methods for doing research, writing, and learning Japanese. We met and talked numerous times during the following years and I was delighted that he decided to do it the right way: to become an apprentice of a true soba master and to take the time to go deep and learn the old ways.

Buckwheat has been cultivated in Japan for over 1,100 years, and soba (buckwheat noodles) has been made for more than 300 years. While studying soyfoods in Japan, I observed that behind every classical Japanese food is both an ancient tradition and a time-honored craft. For masters of this craft, it is a deep daily practice, for some even a spiritual practice, that nourishes both the craftsman and those who partake of his food.

James Udesky is the first Westerner to become a soba master. Thus, this book is a rich source of original information, based on a three-year apprenticeship, careful study and translation of Japanese documents on soba, and extensive contacts with experts in the field. Another rich realm of Japanese food culture has been transmitted to the West. And the timing has been excellent, for there is currently a revival of interest in buckwheat and soba in America and the world.

During the late 1960s and the 1970s in America and Europe, natural food and macrobiotic companies (such as Chico-San, Erewhon, Westbrae, Eden, and Lima) began to import soba and publicize its many virtues. Although most Japanese soba presently contains 20 to 40 percent buckwheat flour (the rest is wheat flour), these companies reintroduced the traditional type containing 80 percent or more buckwheat flour. Many natural-food stores now also sell buckwheat groats and flour.

In addition, nutritionists have come to recognize the importance of whole grains and complex carbohydrates in Western diets that are so overloaded with saturated fats and cholesterol (largely from meat) that large numbers of adults die of coronary heart disease. In the world's three great pasta countries (China, Japan, and Italy), where grains are still a major part of the diet, rates of heart disease are low. Happily, in America pasta has risen to the status of an "in" food.

Finally, agronomists are realizing that buckwheat— a plant which grows well in poor, dry, marginal soil, even in far northern or southern latitudes with short growing seasons—provides solid nutrition and can play a key role in feeding more and more people on less and less land. Here is an under-utilized plant whose time has come.

What Johnny Appleseed did for apples, James Udesky is doing for buckwheat and for soba. May he be equally successful!

William Shurtleff

Introduction

Among the main foods featured in traditional Japanese cuisine, sushi, tofu, and miso are now receiving widespread attention around the world. People concerned with their weight, cholesterol level, or blood pressure, for example, are looking to the "wisdom of the East" for clues on how to solve these problems from a dietary point of view.

At the same time that these foods are becoming accepted, soba cuisine (buckwheat noodles), a veritable giant within the world of traditional Japanese foods, is just now beginning to receive its due share of notice and appreciation in the West.

Having had a seven-year background in the natural foods previous to going to Japan, I was well prepared to discover, explore, and learn the secrets of Japanese original cuisine. Although I had eaten and grown accustomed to the natural sweetness of such grains as brown rice, wheat, and corn, I had never realized that buckwheat and noodles made from freshly hulled and still-moist buckwheat flour could produce such a refreshing and sweet taste. Not, that is, until I had a chance invitation to go to a soba restaurant which serves handmade noodles from freshly ground flour.

Soba cuisine has enjoyed widespread popularity for

over 400 years in Japan. One of the main reasons for this continued popularity is that its light, sweet taste, together with its substantial, energy-giving kilocalories, make soba a perfect food for any season. During the hot summer months when the heat drains your energy and appetite, a light snappy tray of cool soba noodles served with freshly grated horseradish and a chilled but well-balanced dipping sauce constitutes a meal that revitalizes you and actually helps stimulate your appetite. On the other hand, during the cold winter months when you need a food to provide warmth and energy, Tempura Soba, Curry Soba, or other soba dishes served in a hot broth settle you down and hit the spot.

The word *soba* refers to "long and thin brownish noodles" served plain or in soup. It is also the Japanese word for buckwheat, the plant and even the whole kernel or groat itself. Often thought of as a grain, botanically speaking buckwheat is classified outside the family of staple grains (Gramineae) which includes wheat, rice, barley, rye, and oats, among others (see About Soba.) Because of its ability to grow from seed to mature kernel in only 75 days and to grow in even barren soil, historically, buckwheat has been of vital importance in times of famine. However, in an ideal environment, such as Nagano Prefecture in Japan, where it is often foggy, the temperature rarely exceeds 68°F even during the summer, and there is enough wind and insect-life for cross-pollination, the buckwheat will produce soba noodles so sweet that they seem to have sugar mixed in. Of course there is none.

From the time that the buckwheat grain is harvested until the time that the long, thin, and sweet noodles are

THE BOOK OF SOBA

delicately placed on top of a finely lacquered tray, buckwheat goes through a "beating" like no other noodle. The name given to this process, *te-uchi*, literally means "beating the buckwheat dough by hand."

Quite different from spaghetti, ramen, *udon*, and other noodles made from wheat flour, buckwheat flour noodles will not stretch easily. In fact, when making buckwheat noodles from 90 to 100 percent buckwheat flour (a technique called *kiko-uchi*, or "pure soba"), you can hear the sound of the rolling pin being pushed into the dough and against the rolling board in quite a forceful and commanding way. You can tell without looking that the buckwheat dough is indeed going through a beating.

Keeping pace with soba's long history, the market for soba has grown considerably. In addition to the 6,000-plus factories making soba noodles on a large scale, there are over 40,000 shops which serve buckwheat noodles to the public. Of these 40,000, approximately 7,000 shops are in Tokyo. Breaking this figure down further, it would not be far off to estimate that out of these 7,000 shops less than 10 percent claim to offer handmade soba noodles. Still, of these 700, it is safe to say that only about 100 to 150 of these shops at most really perform the entire process by hand.

The previous breakdown is necessary because it must be clearly understood from the beginning that all soba noodles are not the same. The places I visited and was apprenticed to fall into the last category. Within this world of soba, one finds masters spicier than their trusty *wasabi*. This is especially true of my first teacher Takeo Abe, owner of the Take Yabu restaurant in Kashiwa, near Tokyo. Upon entering his shop, you are seated on a raised tatami platform and handed the menu by the owner himself. On my first visit, my companion and I ordered one cool dish and one hot one apiece. Like any great artist, Abe watched us closely as the first order of *Natto Soba* was delivered. This dish featured freshly rolled and cut noodles, topped with fragrantly fermented soybeans (*natto*), seasoned with a pinch of ground sesame seeds. Alongside were thin, delicate shavings of bonito, crispy flakes of *nori* seaweed, razor-thin slices of scallion-type onions, and a deep orange egg yolk crowning the center. Accompanying this colorful arrangement was the soba master's famed dipping sauce. Served chilled, it has a sophisticatedly rich and hearty taste.

Mixing the ingredients together, we glanced at each other with apprehension. Soon we were both smiling. Here was food that was as refreshing and light as a salad, yet sweet and energy giving. The firm, light, and slippery texture of the noodles provided a distinctly clean feeling, with a sweet aftertaste. Yet above all, it was the balance between the wholesome buckwheat, the sensual "bacon-like" fragrance of the broth, and the combination and variety of ingredients which was so appealing.

This balance was not there by chance. The dipping sauce, for example, used high-quality bonito stock (boiled 45 minutes), and then combined it with just the right amount of carefully selected soy sauce, *mirin* (Japanese cooking sherry), and sugar to complement the soba. Once blended, the dipping sauce is allowed to sit for three days, as it mellows like wine, saké, soy sauce, and miso.

Right then and there, as the master was clearing our dishes, I declared to him that I must learn how to make this kind of food. He responded enthusiastically, and said that he would give me the opportunity to learn everything. This meant not merely how to make the noodles and the soup, but, more importantly, how to create the proper mood for the customer to appreciate this cuisine. It also included a commitment to an apprenticeship, which required daily practice sessions until the body could move with precision, quickness, and rhythm. The feeling for this rhythm, as well as the mental and physical stamina needed, cannot be acquired overnight.

I agreed to a six-month trial period, and ended up continuing my actual training for three years, at a total of three shops. During this period, I collected books and magazines, newspaper articles, anything I could get my hands on to learn more about the tradition, nutrition, and history of soba. Occasionally I happened upon articles about the buckwheat situation around the world, and was able to catch a glimpse of its long history in Europe, Asia, and America. Obviously, what had so fascinated me was nothing less than a giant of a food, steeped in close to four centuries of tradition.

Today, modern science is shedding new light on the verifiable, nutritional value of traditional foods, and the important role they can play as part of our daily diet. Added to the recent resurgence in a high-fiber, low-fat pasta diet, soba provides a gourmet touch to pasta cuisine.

Having the opportunity to study with and observe some of the most earnest practitioners in the field, while living in the country where buckwheat cuisine still holds an undeniable appeal to people of all ages, kindled an irrepressible desire to communicate successfully and reveal the wonder of fresh buckwheat, and the noodles which are produced from its flour. Hopefully, this book will, in like fashion, kindle other people's curiosity, and help them to discover and partake of this valuable nutritional food source.

I
MAKING
SOBA

Homemade Soba Noodles

Making soba noodles at home can be fun, creative, and once you get the hang of it, quite an easy thing to do. By using the utensils and space available in the average kitchen, and by obtaining obtain the freshest buckwheat flour available, you can make fresh buckwheat noodles that will delight and satisfy your family, friends, and guests.

The process will be described in an easy-to-follow, step-by-step method. In the beginning, let this serve as a guide. Later, use it as a springboard for developing your own methods. With each batch, try to improve your technique, speed, and sense of rhythm. After several attempts, you'll gain a measure of confidence, and from then on you'll find yourself looking for any occasion to whip up a fresh batch of noodles for an impromptu lunch or dinner party.

Keep in mind that the two most important elements for making successful soba noodles are obtaining fresh and sufficiently sifted flour, and then performing the initial mixing of the water into the flour in such a way as to allow the buckwheat to develop its own viscosity.

INGREDIENTS **Makes 2¹/₂ pounds (1.1 kg)**

5¹/₄ *cups buckwheat flour* (700 g)*
2¹/₄ *cups wheat flour (300 g)*
   2 *cups water (480 cc)*

EQUIPMENT

Cutting board
Rolling pin
Broad, well-sharpened kitchen knife
Plastic wrap
Large mixing bowl
Strainers

*For the beginner, a ratio of 3 parts wheat to 7 parts buckwheat is recommended. You might even have to settle for a 4 to 6 ratio if the flour is not so fresh and hence lacks binding power. By using more wheat, you are able to take advantage of its gluten to help the flour bind together. As you become more adept and gain more confidence try a 2–8 variation.

Another trick of the trade to increase the binding of the flour is to use boiling water in the initial mixing stages (about 80 percent of the total water used). This is to compensate for the absence of gluten in buckwheat flour. The boiling water quickly penetrates buckwheat's superior starch components as well as activating the binding power of its water-soluble proteins.

When using cold water, there are many other common variations used to supplement the binding power of the buckwheat. One is to beat an egg or two into the cold water before mixing it into the flour, while another is to mix grated mountain yam into the flour before adding the water. Other traditional methods in Japan include adding powdered burdock leaves, used for their elasticity, and soaked and mashed soybeans (see Soy-Soba Noodles, page 90). Experiment developing your own "special blend" of preferred ingredients.

Step 1

Combine the buckwheat and wheat flour in the mixing bowl. While mixing the flour together in a circular motion, add the water little by little. It is important to work quickly, adding 90 percent of the water within the first 30 to 45 seconds. The aim is to avoid forming any large clumps.

Using both hands, mix the moistened and unmoistened flour together. Don't worry about the binding of the flour at this stage.

Step 2

Using the palms and fingertips of both hands, quickly and rhythmically press the flour between your hands. Let the flour pass through your fingers and fall back into the bowl. Repeat until all of the flour feels evenly moistened and starts to form small "pebbles."

THE BOOK OF SOBA

Follow the three-part sequence below:

A: Grab some flour with each hand and close your fingers around it to press.

B: Open up your hand. You should find that the mixture has developed some viscosity.

C: Break this clump apart with your fingers and allow the bigger pebbles of dough to fall back into the bowl. Repeat this sequence 20 to 30 times (over a 2-minute period) with the remaining flour.

The purpose of repeating these quick hand movements is to help the flour develop viscosity. As mysterious as it is strong, buckwheat's viscosity takes some coaxing. In scientific parlance this is referred to as "tapping" the binding power of the water-soluble proteins. Professional soba makers refer to the stage when the viscosity becomes apparent as the "blossoming" of the dough. That is, the individual grains of flour have bound together and "blossomed" into pebble-sized clumps. In essence, in the first three steps you are taking pains to bring about the blossoming and to "build up" a dough that is not just sticky, but one which will be firm, compact, binding, and smooth throughout. If your dough meets these four conditions, you can confidently expect to make a firm and elastic noodle.

STEP 4

Now that the base has been established, add the remaining water and repeat step 3 for 1 minute to mix. The pebbles will expand. The flour's viscosity is gradually "sprouting," causing it to bind together in increasingly larger pebbles.

STEP 5

Next, these pebbles must be kneaded together to form one large ball of dough. Lean over and push down with extended arms on the dough, using the force of your back and shoulders (especially that of the shoulder-blade area). Knead the dough with a pumping motion, left-right-left-right for 1 to 2 minutes.

Pack the dough together. Knead the portion of dough closest to you five to ten times, rotate 90°, and knead again. Rotate and knead until the dough is smooth throughout.

STEP 6

Roll the dough around the inside of the bowl to prevent air pockets from forming, then flatten.

STEP 7

Break the dough into 5 or 6 little balls and place them in another bowl. Cover with a damp cloth to prevent the dough from drying out (it dries quickly). Working with 1 ball at a time, roll it between your hands to smooth "from inside to out." Though sticky in the beginning, as you continue kneading it will become smooth and polished. When dough is firm, roll it into a ball.

STEP 8

Spread a little buckwheat flour over the surface of the cutting board and place a single, well-kneaded ball on top. Sprinkle with a little flour. Press down to flatten, then rotate and press to form a flat disc of dough.

With the rolling pin, roll out into an oval with a thickness of approximately ⅛ inch (3 millimeters). The length should be about twice the width. Sprinkle with buckwheat flour as necessary to prevent sticking.

Sprinkle buckwheat flour on a piece of plastic wrap, lay the rolled-out dough on the plastic, and wrap it up. Repeat with the remaining balls of dough, placing each new flattened oval on top of the previous one. Sprinkle flour between each layer to prevent sticking.

STEP 9

When all the balls have been rolled out, return the stacked layers to the cutting board. Cut the layers in half and stack neatly, cut ends aligned. Fold in half.

To cut, place the left palm on the dough and "shave" off ⅛-inch-wide noodles with the knife, moving it forward and through the dough.

Cooking the Noodles

When cooking soba noodles use an ample amount of water. As is true of other types of noodles, there is really no such thing as too much water, but too little water may, among other things, cause noodles to cling together or otherwise cook improperly. In general, the following is recommended:

For $\frac{1}{4}$ pound (115 g) of noodles use
    2 quarts of water (1.6 liters)
For $\frac{1}{2}$ pound (225 g), $2\frac{1}{2}$ quarts (2 liters)
For 1 pound (450 g),   4 quarts (3.2 liters)

Since there is perhaps a limit to the capacity of pots ordinarily at hand, use more than one pot or do the noodles in batches when cooking large amounts.

In determining whether a pot is too large or small, a rule of thumb suggests the true capacity of a pot to be 80 percent at most. Just keep in mind, the bigger the better.

STEP 1
Bring the water to a rolling boil. Add the noodles and stir gently back and forth, being particularly careful when using fresh noodles.

STEP 2

Soon after the noodles are put into the water, their starch begins to dissolve. This causes the water to become milky and a foam to form and swell to the top.

FOR FRESH NOODLES: Control the foam by lowering the flame. Be ready to lower it to a medium flame as soon as the water begins to rise. Once lowered, cook with the water-level near to but just shy of the rim for about 1 to $1\frac{1}{2}$ minutes.

FOR DRIED NOODLES: When the foam starts to swell, add a $\frac{1}{2}$ cup (120 cc) of cold water and lower the heat slightly. Repeat this procedure twice. When the water comes to a boil for the third time, test the noodles (see the next step). If they are done, turn off the heat and remove from the stove.

STEP 3

To test, occasionally lift a few noodles from the pot. Finished noodles should be served *al dente*; that is, tender but firm and chewy throughout. Press or taste noodles frequently. Remember, if the noodles are to be served in a hot broth, they should be a bit firmer when taken out (and allowed to finish "cooking" in the broth).

STEP 4

Pour the noodles into a strainer, capturing the cooking water in another pot. Reserve a portion of the cooking water, or *soba-yu* (which contains valuable water-soluble proteins and other minerals), if the recipe calls for it. Remove the noodles to a large bowl of ice water to firm them up. When the noodles have cooled somewhat, stir briskly for 5 to 10 seconds to "wash" the starch off. Rinse well.

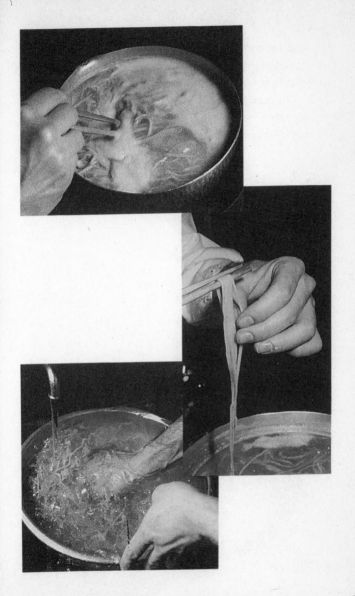

HOMEMADE SOBA NOODLES

STEP 5

To cool or chill the noodles, douse in cold water just before serving. Use ice water in summer. Drain well.

To reheat the noodles, place them in a strainer and dip in hot cooking water (reheat if necessary) for 20 to 30 seconds. Drain well, especially if served on a plate.

Serve according to the instructions for each recipe.

The Professional Method

The three main steps of mixing, rolling, and cutting are the same in both the professional and home methods. At the professional shop, a lacquered mixing bowl is used to give a nice smooth finish to the ball of dough. A fine cypress roller and two longer wrapping pins are used to handle the large sheet of dough. A tall knife is used in combination with a board (komaita) to ensure even cutting through 12 to 16, or as many as 20, layers of dough.

1

2

3

4

11 12

13 14

15 16

17

18

19

20

21

22

23

Broth

Either a hot or cold broth accompanies a portion of soba noodles. A bowl of hot noodles is served in a piping hot broth, a plate or "basket" of cold noodles with a dipping sauce. Aside from the temperature at which they are served and infinite regional variations, the main difference between the two "broths" lies in the strength: the cold version has approximately three times the flavor base of its hot counterpart.

The dipping sauce, which developed mainly in Kanto, the eastern region of Japan (around Tokyo), is served in small portions (usually a small ladleful) within a nicely decorated and rather petite cup known as a *choko*. It has a wonderfully refreshing and stimulating bite that complements the modest but pure, clean taste of buckwheat.

The hot soup, developed mainly in Kansai, the western region of Japan (around Kyoto and Osaka), is usually served in large bowls with hot soba noodles. As implied by its Kansai nickname, *ama-jiru* (sweet or mild broth), it is meant to be pleasing to the last drop without leaving a salty aftertaste.

It is said that no two soba shops in Japan make exactly the same broth. This belief, exaggerated or not, illustrates the fact that many elements are at play in determining the final taste. Although the two most obvious of these seem to be the quality and ratio of ingredients, other subtle but undeniable factors contribute to the variety of broths. One often-cited factor is the time involved in cooking down the broth. The professionals judge when a broth is done not by how long it has cooked but by how much it has decreased in volume, since the cooking time varies according to the flame, the thickness of the pot, and other variables. From this we can take the hint that it is the volume of stock combined with just the right volume of flavor base that is one of the most fundamental factors in creating a delicious soup to accompany soba.

Four different soba broths are given here. These recipes represent the standard methods of preparation which have been passed down through the centuries, and yield soups which splendidly complement the taste of soba.

Recipe I—a professional method for making a large quantity of flavor base that can be kept indefinitely and continues to mature the longer it is kept.

Recipe II—a scaled-down version of the first recipe that matures in 6 to 8 hours.

Recipe III—an instant broth.

Recipe IV—a sugarless broth for those on restricted diets.

As you become more comfortable in their preparation, feel free to make adjustments in your search for the taste which best matches your individual or family needs.

For those who are on restricted salt diets, any of the stocks (minus the flavor base) suggested in these recipes will yield a satisfying hot soup. For a saltless chilled soup, allow this same stock to cool and then combine with fresh, "in-season" fruit puree or broths taken from cooked vegetables to suit your dietary needs, or follow the suggestions below.

Expanding Your Repertoire of Soba Broths

Although the following recommended broths are traditional favorites, there is no reason why the stock must be limited only to bonito and/or *konbu* kelp. Since the sweet, mild taste of buckwheat is, like tofu, subtle and sophisticated, it lends itself well to almost any combination of ingredients. The main point, after all, is to enhance your diet by eating buckwheat.

So, for those who want to experiment, the field is wide open. If you love chicken soup or beef bouillon, try making your favorite broths and then adding the flavor base at the end.

For variations on the chilled dipping sauce, you might blend the chilled variety in a food processor together with soft fruits such as avocados or bananas. Or, to attain a nutty fragrance, combine it with walnuts, peanuts, or the like. Try spicing it with ginger or finely chopped celery. Served with chilled fresh noodles, this combination will not only revive almost any flagging appetite but will help to ease those summertime blues.

RECIPE I

A Professional Broth

In the soba shop, the master makes his broth or dipping sauce by combining that day's stock with a bit of his own blend of flavor base. He prepares the base days or months in advance and allows it to mature—like good wine.

There are many advantages to making the flavor base and broth separately. Once made and properly stored (storage is described in detail below), the base will keep indefinitely. This enables it to be used with great flexibility and convenience. For example, merely by altering the ratio between the base and the basic stock (also explained below), you can make either the hot soup or the chilled dipping sauce. That is, when you want to make a fresh broth, you need only prepare a basic stock and combine it with the "ready-made" base. In addition, this method allows you easily to adjust the strength of the soup by simply altering the base/stock ratio.

A further advantage is that, having this flavor base on hand, you will find many ways to sneak it into your cooking—for example, using it as a flavoring agent for a teriyaki sauce, brushing it over fried or baked chicken, or adding that "extra" taste to stews, breads, or cooked vegetables.

Another benefit of a separate base is that, as in the fermentation process which takes place in wine- and miso-making, the "edge" (that is, the salt in the soy sauce and the sugar) is softened and allowed to "ferment" for at least 3 days before using (although at a pinch it can be used after 12 hours). Thus, it develops a well-balanced taste and takes on a nature greater than the sum of its parts.

BASE

> 1 qt soy sauce *(800 cc)*
> ³⁄₄ cup mirin *(180 cc)*
> ³⁄₅ cup sugar* *(150 g)*

Combine the soy sauce and *mirin* in a heavy-bottomed pot and heat over a medium flame. Take special pains to dry the pot completely with a towel, as even a drop of water will endanger the proper storing ability of this base.

When a white foam starts to form on the surface, add the sugar, lower the flame a touch, and stir continuously with a wooden spoon to prevent the sugar from sticking to the bottom. The sugar will dissolve and the white foam will again begin to form. When it covers about 50 percent of the surface (professionals will allow it to go to 80 or 90 percent), remove the pot from the stove. Although it is permissible to allow the liquid to boil slightly at the rim, watch the liquid closely and do not let it reach a full boil.

It is essential that not even a hint of water be allowed to enter into the process. Before placing it in a storage container, allow the base to sit overnight in a cool, dark place. Cover with a cloth, towel, or newspaper (water will condense on a pot lid or other nonabsorbent cover).

At the traditional shops this base is allowed to mature and mellow for 3 full days before using. As the quantities called for in this recipe are tailored to a home scale, a minimum maturing period of 12 hours (overnight) is more than sufficient, although 2 to 3 days will produce a superior flavor.

Store in a closed container in a cool, dark place.

*Combined with the recommended stock, the flavor base in this recipe will provide enough soup for 68 portions of dipping sauce or about 30 portions of the hot variety (depending on the strength). This means that there will only be about a pinch (2.2 grams) of sugar in a portion of the chilled soup, and about 5 grams in a portion of the hot.

Making the Stock

As stocks using *konbu* kelp will cloud if allowed to sit for more than 24 hours, make only as much stock as you will use on that day. Nevertheless, these recipes will yield slightly more than the "standard volume," to ensure that you will not come up short.

HOT STOCK **Serves 6**

4–6 *inch length* konbu *kelp (optional) (10–12 cm)*
8 *cups water (1.9 liters)*
1½–2 *oz bonito flakes (40–55g)*

CHILLED STOCK

2 *inch length* konbu *kelp (optional) (5 cm)*
1½ *cups water (360 cc)*
⅔–1 *oz bonito flakes (18–28 g)*

Wipe the kelp lightly with a dry cloth and combine with water in a wide-mouthed pot. Cook over low heat for 3 minutes. To ensure a thicker and tastier broth, leave the kelp in for 1 to 2 minutes after the broth reaches a boil. Then remove it, discard, and turn up the heat to medium-high.

When the stock starts to boil in earnest, add the bonito flakes. Skim off the white foam and continue boiling over low heat for about 10 to 15 minutes.

When the broth has boiled down to about two-thirds of its original volume, turn off the flame. In one motion, pour the broth into a cloth-covered strainer. If you do this too slowly, the fragrance of the bonito is said to diminish noticeably.

At this point, there are two schools of thought. In standard Japanese cooking, to prevent the slightly astringent, "fishy" taste of the bonito from dominating, the cloth containing the wet flakes is not wrung out. Yet, this quality is actually desired by the soba-maker, and hence by and large the practice of thoroughly squeezing the cooked flakes occurs. Experiment and decide which method you want to follow.

Making the Broth

The stock and flavor base are combined in ratios that have been passed down through the centuries. If you find the results too weak or strong, however, feel free to make suitable adjustments.

HOT BROTH
   1   part flavor base
   8–10   parts stock

DIPPING SAUCE
   1   part flavor base
   3   parts stock

Combine stock and base in required amounts. Heat over a medium-high flame until the broth *starts* to boil at the rim of the pot. Reduce the heat immediately and simmer for 10 to 15 minutes. If you are making hot broth, it is ready to be served.

The chilled dipping sauce, however, obviously must be cooled before serving. This can be done in two ways. The best way is to allow it to cool naturally for about 2 to 3 hours, and then cover and refrigerate it until it reaches about 50°F or, in summertime, 40°F. (As in the maturing process of the flavor base, the chilled broth is said to "ripen to its fullest" if allowed to cool naturally.) When time is short, the broth can be "force-cooled" after it has been allowed to cool naturally for about 10 minutes. To do this, place the pot of broth in a larger pot or bowl filled with ice water and stir until it reaches the above temperature.

RECIPE II
A Professional Broth at Home

Here is a professional recipe that can be made on a smaller scale. Although the basic principle is the same as in Recipe I, by practicing with the lesser amounts given here, you can gain confidence and also determine what adjustments (if any) you would like to make to the standard recipe before making the larger amount of flavor base. In addition, since the scale is smaller, the flavor base will mature quicker and be ready to serve 6 to 8 hours after making. You could easily make it in the morning for an evening soba party.

FLAVOR BASE   **Yields about 9 cups (2.16 liters)**[*]

    $1\frac{1}{2}$ cups soy sauce *(360 cc)*
     $\frac{1}{4}$ cup mirin *(60 cc)*
     $\frac{1}{4}$ cup sugar *(65 g)*

COLD FLAVOR BASE

    $2\frac{1}{8}$ cups soy sauce *(510 cc)*
     7   *Tbsps* mirin
     6   *Tbsps* sugar *(90 g)*

STOCK

    $7\frac{1}{2}$ cups water *(1.8 liters)*
  $1\frac{1}{2}$–3   oz bonito flakes *(40–85 g)*

Make the flavor base following the instructions in the previous recipe. Allow to mature for 6 to 8 hours. Combine the broth ingredients following the procedure given in Recipe I (omitting the steps for *konbu* kelp).

RECIPE III
Instant Broth

This recipe is the easiest and quickest of the first three, but has been placed last so that by now you will thoroughly understand the principle do's and don'ts of making a successful soba soup. Although it is meant for immediate use, this broth, like the flavor bases of the earlier recipes, benefits if it is allowed to sit for a time, in this case overnight.

CHILLED DIPPING SAUCE   **Serves 4**

5	inch piece konbu *kelp (12 cm)*
½	cup soy sauce *(120 cc)*
2	cups water *(480 cc)*
2–3	oz bonito flakes *(55–85 g)*
3½	Tbsps mirin
2½	Tbsps sugar

HOT BROTH

5	inch piece konbu *kelp (12 cm)*
8	cups water *(1.92 liters)*
3–4	oz bonito flakes *(80–100 g)*
1	cup soy sauce *(240 cc)*
5	Tbsps mirin
4	Tbsps sugar

Wipe the kelp with a damp cloth and place in the water. Bring the water to a boil at high heat.

When the water comes to a boil, remove the kelp and immediately add the bonito flakes. Reduce the heat to medium and allow the water to boil for 3 minutes, stirring and pushing down the shavings with a wooden spoon.

Reduce to a low flame and add the soy sauce, *mirin*, and sugar. Cook for an additional 5 minutes. Stir gently to prevent the sugar from sticking to the bottom and to bring out the full taste of the bonito flakes.

Pour the finished broth through a cloth-covered strainer.

RECIPE IV

A Sugarless Broth

2–3	oz bonito flakes (55–85 g)	**Serves 4**
4	cups water (960 cc)	
1	cup soy sauce (240 cc)	
³⁄₄	cup mirin (180 cc)	

Place the bonito and water in a pot, and heat over a high flame.

When the broth starts to boil, a white foam will form on the surface. Skim off the foam and lower the heat to medium-low for about 2 minutes. The flame should be just hot enough to keep the shavings aloft and moving around.

Pour through a cloth-covered strainer, then return to the stove. Turn the flame to high. When the broth begins to boil at the rim of the pot, add the soy sauce and *mirin*. Return to a boil, turn off the heat, and remove the pot from the stove.

For the hot broth, serve as is. For the chilled broth, allow to cool as for standard dipping sauce (page 49).

Noodle Dishes

Soba Noodles in a Basket
Mori / Zaru / Seiro Soba

This is the simplest and yet "most dangerous" dish on the soba master's menu. In Japan, it is also the most popular. Since only the dipping sauce and the humblest of garnishes accompany it, the noodle must stand on its own merits. To the connoisseur of soba, this is the most delicious way—some say the only way—to savor buckwheat's sweetness. *Mori Soba* and the *nori*-topped *Zaru Soba* are extremely popular on a hot summer day, and interestingly enough, are often served at the end of a banquet or party-style dinners where the guests have had a lot to drink. Not only does soba help to lower the blood pressure but it also aids the liver in dealing with the alcohol. Combining the cooking water, which contains much of the water-soluble protein, with the remaining dipping sauce to make a soup is a satisfying final touch.

The roots of the Japanese name of this dish reach back well over 300 years to a time when the work of making soba noodles was entrusted to the local confectioner. Since noodles made from 100-percent buckwheat are prone to break easily, sweet makers steamed

Soba Noodles in a Basket

and then served the noodles in bamboo baskets, or *take zaru*. Today, wheat flour mixed in with the buckwheat gives the dough a binding power that makes it possible to boil the noodles, yet the tradition of putting them out in bamboo baskets continues, as does the name.

Serves 3–4

1¼ lbs homemade soba noodles (480–600 g)
  or
1 lb dried soba noodles (450 g)
1 cup dipping sauce (240 cc)
  or
5½ Tbsps flavor base and 1¼ cups stock (300 cc)
1 sheet nori *seaweed (optional), cut into thin strips*
2 *scallions, finely sliced*
2 tsps wasabi *horseradish*
4 Tbsps grated daikon *radish*

Make the dipping sauce of your choice (pages 43–52) and chill it (page 49).

Boil and wash the noodles (pages 34–38), reserving about one-third of the cooking water. Drain well.

Place the noodles on plates or in traditional *zaru* baskets and garnish with strips of *nori*. Set out the dipping sauce for each person. Season sauce to taste with scallion, *wasabi*, and grated daikon. Serve immediately.

When you have finished eating the noodles, reheat the cooking water and top off the remaining dipping sauce to make a soup.

Hot Soba Noodles in a Broth
Kake Soba

This is a hot version at its most basic. Originally served with a lukewarm soup as a quick, nutritious meal for hurried laborers and craftsmen of the early seventeenth century, this simple and satisfying meal still enjoys an immense following among those on the run. Try topping the noodles with a quarter sheet of *nori* seaweed crowned with salmon roe caviar (*ikura*).

Serves 3–4

1¼	lbs homemade soba noodles (480–600 g)
	or
1	lb dried soba noodles (450 g)
6	cups broth (1.45 liters)
	or
½	cup flavor base (120 cc) and 4½ cups stock (1.1 liters)
1½	Tbsps grated ginger
2	scallions, finely sliced

Make the broth of your choice (pages 43–52).

Boil, wash, and reheat the noodles (pages 34–38), but remove them before they are *al dente*. The noodles should be about 90 percent done (they will finish cooking when placed in the hot broth). Wash and strain, then set aside in a strainer.

Reheat the broth over high heat, and at the same time reheat the cooking water. When the broth shows the first signs of boiling at the rim of the pot, remove from heat. Reheat the noodles one at a time by placing in the strainer and dipping in the hot cooking water.

Place the noodles in serving bowls. Cover with the hot broth, garnish with ginger and scallion, and serve immediately.

VARIATION: A simpler recipe calls for the noodles to be served in their steaming-hot cooking water, which contains some of buckwheat's water soluble proteins and other nutrients. The noodles are dipped in a hot dipping sauce, with a 3 to 1 ratio of stock to flavor base.

Cold Soba Noodles with Grated Radish

This dish is particularly refreshing on a sultry summer afternoon. The zesty daikon (choose as spicy a one as you can find) serves to whet lagging appetites. Don't hold back on the bonito flakes or ground sesame, the latter of which lessens the slight astringency of the flakes.

Serves 3–4

1¼ lbs homemade soba noodles (480–600 g)
or
1 lb dried soba noodles (450 g)
1–1¼ cups dipping sauce (240–300 cc)
or
7 Tbsps flavor base and 1¼ cups stock (300 cc)
2 tsps fresh sesame seeds
2 cups grated daikon radish (substitute any large white radish)
2 scallions, finely sliced
1 sheet nori seaweed, toasted and shredded
4 heaped Tbsps bonito flakes
Soy sauce

Make the broth of your choice (pages 43–52) and cool (page 49).

Toast the sesame seeds in a dry frypan over medium heat until they begin to emit a nut-like fragrance, then remove *immediately* from the pan. Grind with a mortar and pestle.

Boil, wash, and cool the noodles (pages 34–38), reserving the water.

Drain the noodles well and place in individual serving bowls. Squeeze out excess water from the grated radish, then mound on top of the noodles. Sprinkle the scallion, *nori*, bonito flakes, and finally sesame around the daikon. Pour a small amount of soy sauce over the radish. Set out individual portions of dipping sauce. Add sliced scallions to sauce as desired. When you have finished the noodles, reheat the cooking water and top off the remaining sauce to make a soup.

Tempura Soba

Ask any master of a high-class soba restaurant what the most popular dish on his menu is, and most likely Tempura Soba will get the nod. Basically there are three types, each a variation along the soba noodle–tempura axis.

The most common version calls for large shrimp to be dipped in tempura batter and deep-fried, tail and all. These are set right on top of a bed of hot noodles floating in broth. Another version combines shrimp or assorted tempura with Soba Noodles in a Basket, and is called *Tenzaru*. (To make, simply follow this recipe but serve the noodles cold with a dipping sauce. The tempura becomes a side dish.) The last variety is an attractive, mixed-fry tempura "patty." This is likewise set on top of hot noodles or served on its own tray when accompanying cold noodles (see the following recipe).

First timers seem to like the tempura served on its own separate dish, as it retains its crispy quality. Others prefer the rich taste and body-warming feeling that is produced by allowing the tempura to melt into the soup.

With any of these types, the tempura should be served almost immediately after cooking. If it is allowed to sit for more than 2 or 3 minutes, its crispiness is lost. Ideally, the tempura should be hot enough to make a sizzling, crackling sound as it is placed into the hot broth. At the high-class restaurants this sizzling sound will still be audible when it is placed in front of you!

1¼	lbs homemade soba noodles (600 g)	**Serves 4**
	or	
1	lb dried soba noodles (450 g)	
6	cups hot broth (1.45 liters)	
	or	
10	Tbsps flavor base and 6 cups stock (1.45 liters)	

TEMPURA*

    8   large shrimp
1½   cups all-purpose flour
    1   cup cold water (240 cc)
    1   egg yolk
        Oil for deep-frying

Make the broth of your choice (pages 43–52).

Prepare the shrimp: remove the outer shell, trim the middle prong of the tail but leave the 2 outer ones. Rinse the shrimp in salt water. Devein by making a lengthwise insertion along the back and removing the blackish material with a toothpick. Furthermore, make 3 shallow incisions horizontally along the underside so that the cooked shrimp will lay flat (that is, it will not curl up when placed into the oil). Run the dull edge of the knife along the tail to force out any excess water from the tail fins. Pat the shrimp dry.

Combine the egg yolk with 1 cup water and whip briskly for about 3 to 5 seconds. Sift in the flour and stir gently in a "figure 8" 2 or 3 times. This will be enough to ensure a proper blending. The final batter should look incompletely mixed. Too much stirring will activate the gluten within the wheat and create a sticky, paste-like batter, which is not suitable for making good tempura. (The technique in mixing the batter is similar to that of the tofu maker's method of stirring *nigari* into the heated soybean juice: the idea is not to disturb.) Therefore, stop mixing while a ring of flour remains around the rim.

If the batter drips off the fork in noticeably distinct drops, it is the proper consistency. It shouldn't run off like water, nor should it just stick there.

The proper temperature of the oil can be tested by putting a drop or two of the batter into the oil. If the drop sinks to the bottom, the oil is still too cold. If the first few drops stay on top as soon as they make contact, the oil is too hot. The proper temperature (320°–340°F/160°–170°C) is attained when the drops of batter sink down almost to the bottom and come right back up. Adjust the flame until the proper heat is attained.

Meanwhile, boil and wash the noodles (pages 34–38). Remove to a strainer. Reserve the cooking water to reheat the noodles.

When the noodles are finished, begin the tempura. Pick up the prepared shrimp by holding the tail end with the first two fingers and thumb of either hand. Dip it into the batter, then transfer it quickly but gently to the oil. Cook until the outside is crispy and golden yellow (not brown). The inside, of course, should be cooked but not hard.

While the tempura is cooking, reheat the broth. Remove it from the stove as soon as it begins to boil at the rim.

Reheat the noodles, place them in individual bowls, cover with hot broth, and top with the shrimp. Serve immediately.

*Soba shops use a batter that is slightly thicker than standard tempura batter, so it is allowed to cook a little longer in the oil. Depending on whether someone comes from the Tokyo or Osaka area, their opinion as to what is the best kind of oil will differ. Tokyo style calls for the richer (and more expensive) sesame oil as a base (20 percent). Osaka style relies on a light vegetable oil.

The key point to obtaining a successful tempura is to perform all of the various activities quickly and confidently, so that the noodles will not be finished too far in advance of the tempura, and absolutely not vice versa.

As for the cooking time, please keep in mind that the ingredients to be deep-fried should be so fresh that they can be eaten raw (or nearly so). This is the unspoken assumption of all good tempura chefs. Thus, even if the tempura is a little bit "undercooked," it is not at all a total failure, since the food could have been eaten as it was. By following this practice you need only guard against overcooking. Tempura is meant to be delicate, so avoid a hard, dark-colored finished product.

Incidentally, the professionals judge the tempura not only by sight but also by sound. During the first half-minute or so of deep-frying, the tempura will make a sizzling sound. When it is sufficiently cooked, the sound will become a crackling chorus. When you can distinguish between the two, you know that your tempura-making ability has progressed.

Soba Noodles with Mixed-Fry Tempura

This recipe features a tempura patty and calls for shrimp and scallops, though very often only shrimp are used. The easiest way to prepare this dish is simply to put all the chopped ingredients directly into a rather thick batter and then spoon the mixture into preheated oil (320°–340°F/160°–170°C). A second, more sophisticated method which produces a much lighter result is described below.

1¼	lbs homemade soba noodles (600 g)	**Serves 3–4**
	or	
1	lb dried soba noodles (450 g)	
6	cups hot broth (1.45 liters)	
	or	
10	Tbsps flavor base and 6 cups stock (1.45 liters)	
2	scallions, finely sliced	

TEMPURA

½	lb shrimp (230 g)
3	oz very fresh scallops (80 g)
½	medium onion, chopped
	Oil for deep-frying
1½	cups all-purpose flour
1	egg yolk
1	cup water (240 cc)

Make the broth of your choice (pages 43–52).

Wash and devein the shrimp. Remove the tail. Wash the scallops in lightly salted water. Chop both coarsely.

Boil and wash the noodles (pages 34–38). Reserve the cooking water to reheat the noodles.

Preheat the oil. To test the temperature of oil, see the previous recipe.

Make the batter following the instructions in the previous recipe. In a separate bowl, combine the shrimp, scallops, and chopped onions. Follow one of the two methods for deep-frying.

METHOD A: Thicken the batter with 2 to 3 Tbsps of flour. Then ladle a quarter of the chopped ingredients directly into the batter and coat well. Scoop out the patty of seafood with a spatula and place it into the oil. Shape the patty by dripping

extra batter on top and mounding on any stray pieces. Cook to a light golden color (not brown).

METHOD B: This is a more sophisticated recipe (used by the professionals) and produces a lighter tempura. Find an empty can. It should be about 3 inches (8 cm) in diameter. Cut out the ends, then wash and dry it well. Place it in the preheated oil. Add the chopped ingredients to the batter, mix, and then ladle into the can. Drip a few drops of batter on top, creating a nice "crown" effect. Spoon about 4 or 5 ladles of oil over the top and cook for about 30 seconds. Lift the can from the tempura and cook until the batter turns a light golden color. Repeat this procedure to make three more patties. Before making the remaining patties, test the oil. The patty shape should form within about 10 to 15 seconds and become firm within 30 seconds. Cook about 2 to 3 minutes. Allow the finished tempura to drain for about 5 to 10 seconds before serving.

Reheat the broth. Reheat the noodles by placing them in a strainer and dipping them in hot cooking water. Shake out the extra water, and place them in individual bowls. Cover with the broth, crown with the tempura, garnish with scallion, and serve immediately.

Soba Noodles with Whipped Mountain Yam and Egg

The Japanese mountain yam is undeniably an acquired taste, but once acquired, like many another fine food, it is addictive. It is cool and refreshing and as slippery as oysters in a half shell. Western palates will find the glutinous stickiness of the yam yet another one of those inexplicable Japanese culinary experiences. It has a mild taste, so it responds well when combined with other foods or seasonings, such as the broth in this recipe.

Front to back: Duck and Leek Soba (see Chicken and Leek Soba), Soba Noodles with Whipped Mountain Yam and Egg, "Fox" Soba

1¼	lbs fresh soba noodles (480–600 g)	**Serves 3–4**
	or	
1	lb dried soba noodles (450 g)	
1¼	cups dipping sauce (300 cc)	
	or	
5½	Tbsps flavor base and 1¼ cups stock (300 cc)	
1	medium mountain yam (yama imo)	
1	sheet nori seaweed	
4	egg yolks (optional)	
2	scallions, finely sliced	
2	tsps wasabi horseradish	

Make the dipping sauce of your choice (pages 43–52) and chill (page 49).

Pour half of the chilled sauce into a bowl, and grate half of the yam. Repeat with the remaining broth and yam. Combine both portions and mix well.

Toast the seaweed by passing it back and forth over a high flame several times until it becomes shiny and emits a pleasant fragrance. Tear into bite-sized pieces.

Boil, wash, and strain the noodles (pages 34–38).

Place the noodles in individual bowls. Cup your hand over the noodles and turn the bowl upside down, gently pressing the noodles to squeeze out any remaining water. Top with the grated yam and crown with an egg yolk (if desired). Garnish with nori, scallion, and wasabi. Serve immediately. Mix well before eating.

Cold Soba Noodles with Natto and Sesame

Natto, a kind of fermented soybean product, has a rather strong fragrance and flavor somewhat similar to that of fine cheese. But when "garnished" with the chilled soba broth, the combination exhibits an exotic, almost burgundy-like fragrance and taste which complements buckwheat's modest sweetness. The recipe itself is very easy, but it is important to achieve a proper balance between the *natto*, the other garnishes, and the chilled dipping sauce.

Serves 3–4

1¼	lbs homemade soba noodles (480–600 g)	
	or	
1	lb dried soba noodles (450 g)	
1¼	cups dipping sauce (300 cc)	
	or	
7	Tbsps flavor base and 1¼ cups stock (300 cc)	
²/₃	oz natto	
2	scallions, finely sliced (20 g)	
4	egg yolks (optional)	
4	tsps fresh sesame seeds	
1	sheet nori *seaweed*	
4	heaping tsps bonito flakes	

Make the dipping sauce (pages 43–52) and chill (page 49).

When working with *natto*, its dual nature should be taken into account. On the one hand, *natto* is made from cooked soybeans, which are inherently sweet. Yet, when these cooked soybeans are activated with a fermenting seed and allowed to sit at slightly above room temperature for about 16 to 24 hours, the outer part of the bean takes on a mild, astringent taste, while the center part retains its sweetness. If you are not accustomed to the astringent side of *natto*, you may like to bring out the sweetness of the soybeans as much as possible.

METHOD A (to bring out the sweetness): Make sure the cutting board is dry. To guarantee stability, place a damp towel underneath it. With a heavy knife, dice the *natto* to create a very fine, glutinous texture. Spend 1 to 2 minutes chopping with quick, brisk strokes. Don't be discouraged by *natto*'s stickiness. It is not necessary that the knife be pulled completely free of the beans on the upstroke. The important thing is to mash them thoroughly.

METHOD B: Chop the *natto* briskly for about 20 to 30 seconds into a coarse mix. This activates the *natto* just enough to make it more digestible without destroying the biting effect which real *natto* lovers crave.

Whip the *natto* together into a ball.

Place the sesame seeds in a dry skillet over low heat. Roast, stirring constantly until the seeds begin to emit a nut-like fragrance. Remove immediately from the pan. Grind in a mortar and pestle.

Pass the sheet of *nori* seaweed back and forth over a medium flame several times. Within 10 to 15 seconds, the surface will become shiny and the *nori* will emit a nice fragrance. Turn off the heat and tear the sheet into bite-sized pieces.

Boil, wash, and rinse the noodles (pages 34–38).

Place the noodles in individual bowls and with one hand cupped over the top, turn the bowl upside down and gently press to squeeze out any excess water. Add $1/4$ cup (60 cc) broth. Make a small indentation in the center of noodles, then place in an egg yolk. Garnish with the *nori*, bonito flakes, and sliced onions. Top with *natto*, then sprinkle sesame seeds over *natto*. To eat, mix the ingredients, combining well with the broth.

"Rosy-Cheeked" Soba
Okame Soba

This dish was inspired by the image of the robust working woman of two hundred years past, or so it is said.
Colorful ingredients are playfully arranged to suggest a
woman's face. Pink or pink-bordered slices of fish cake
recall glowing cheeks, for instance. Substitute freely with
whatever you have on hand: sliced carrots for fish cake,
spinach for daikon radish sprouts, and so on. If possible,
cover the dish before you serve it to create an element
of mystery. When the lid is lifted, a fine, steam unveils a
display of delicate garnishes artfully arranged.

Serves 4

- 1¼ lbs homemade soba noodles (480–600 g)
  or
- 1 lb dried soba noodles (450 g)
- 6 cups hot broth (1.45 liters)
  or
- 11 Tbsps flavor base and 6 cups stock (1.45 liters)

THE FACE

- 4 shrimp (hair)
- 1½ oz bamboo shoots (eyes)
- 4 fresh mushrooms (nose)
- 5 Tbsps soy sauce
- 2 Tbsps mirin
- 2 tsps sugar (optional)
- 3 eggs (mouth)
- 8 slices fish cake (kamaboko)
  or
- 8 carrot rounds (cheeks)
- 16 strands daikon radish sprouts (bow)

Make the broth of your choice (pages 43–52).

Wash and devein the shrimp. Boil for 30 seconds.

Cut the bamboo shoots into bite-sized pieces. Remove the stems from the mushrooms. Combine the soy sauce, *mirin*, and sugar with 1 cup broth. Place the mushrooms and bamboo shoots in separate pots and add a portion of broth mixture to each. Bring to a boil and then simmer uncovered until the liquid is absorbed (about 10 minutes).

"Rosy-Cheeked" Soba

THE BOOK OF SOBA

Add 1½ Tbsps (22 cc) flavor base and 3 Tbsps (45 cc) stock to the well-beaten eggs. Whip thoroughly to help create a bubbly texture. Preheat a skillet over medium heat. Lightly oil the pan and add half of the egg dashi mixture. Tap the egg mixture lightly, using chopsticks (or thin shish-kebab-type skewers) to encourage air bubbles to form. When the heat has penetrated but the egg is still moist, fold up in thirds by a combination of flipping the pan (like pancakes) and assisting with chopsticks. Slide to the front of the pan, re-oil the pan, and pour in the remaining egg. Lift the cooked egg (with chopsticks) so that some of the remaining ⅔ of the uncooked egg runs under. Cook and then roll up as before. Form into a block shape by pressing with a spatula. Cut into 1-inch-thick (2 cm) slices. (If you don't have time to make this sensuous oriental egg-dope substitute egg yolks. Place them in the steaming hot broth just before serving so that the yolks are soft-poached by the soup.)

Slice the fish cake, cutting into pieces about a ½ inch thick. By jiggling the knife as you slice forward, you can make appealing designs.

Boil, wash, and reheat the noodles (pages 34–38).

Place the noodles in individual bowls and form the face. Reheat the broth and pour it into the bowl, being careful not to disturb the garnishes. Serve immediately.

Soba Noodles with Tempura Crispies

Tanuki Soba

This dish features deep-fried "crispies," those stray bits of tempura batter that skitter across the oil during the deep-frying. Even so, the shrimp or other tempura ingredients impart some of their flavor to these wayfarers, so leftover crispies work well here. If you do not plan to make tempura in the near future, however, the crispies can be made to order.

Nowadays, people naturally assume that the dish was originally named after the raccoon dog (*tanuki*), whose statue is often found at soba shops. This is in fact not the case. Originally, the Japanese name for the dish was *Tanenuki Soba*. The word *tane-nuki* means "ingredients taken out," and referred, of course, to the tempura batter sans ingredients. The Japanese are fond of punning, and it wasn't long before someone thought to drop the second syllable and call it *Tanuki Soba*, or "Raccoon Dog Soba." Since the raccoon dog is characterized as being a sly and stealthy forager, the humorous, if oblique, reference to shrimp-less tempura has stuck.

Serves 3–4

1¼ lbs homemade soba noodles (480–600 g)
    or
1 lb dried soba noodles (450 g)
6 cups hot broth (1.45 liters)
    or
10 Tbsps flavor base and 6 cups stock (1.45 liters)
8 oz chicken (optional) (220 g)
1–2 scallions, sliced
1 sheet nori seaweed
4 bits citron or lemon zest (optional)

BATTER (if necessary)
    Oil for deep-frying
2 Tbsps water
¼ cup all-purpose white flour (35 g)
1 egg yolk

If you do not have leftover crispies, make up a fresh batch. Preheat the oil to a medium-low deep-frying temperature (340°F/170°C). Mix the batter ingredients roughly (see

Tempura Soba, page 58) and ladle into the oil. During the 1 or 2 minutes of cooking, lightly knock the clumps apart, as small, individual pieces are better. When they attain a nice yellow-golden (not brown) color, scoop them out of the oil and drain on absorbent paper.

Make the broth of your choice (pages 43–52). Heat over a high flame until it begins to boil at the rim. Turn off the heat.

Boil, wash, and strain the noodles (pages 34–38), keeping the boiling water on hand.

Cut the chicken into bite-sized pieces. Slice the scallion at a diagonal into bite-sized pieces.

Pass the sheet of *nori* back and forth over a medium flame several times. Within 10 to 15 seconds, the surface will become shiny and the *nori* will emit a nice fragrance. Turn off the heat and tear the sheet into bite-sized pieces.

Reheat the broth until it begins to boil lightly at the rim of the pot, then add the chicken. When the meat rises to the surface, put in the onion. Cook for 30 seconds, then turn off the flame.

Reheat the noodles by placing them in a strainer and dipping them in the cooking water. (Reheat water if necessary.) Put the noodles in individual serving bowls, arrange the chicken and onions (bunched together) on top of the noodles, and cover with the steaming broth. Sprinkle with the *nori* and garnish with the zest. As the "crispies" soon become soft in the soup broth, add them just before you sit down to eat.

"Fox" Soba

Kitsune Soba

This dish takes its name from an old Japanese folk tale which depicts the fox's keen liking for the squares of deep-fried tofu used in this dish. Light and absorbent, they become juicy, broth-filled morsels when simmered as here.

$1\frac{1}{4}$ lbs homemade soba noodles (480–600 g)
   or
   1 lb dried soba noodles (450 g)
   6 cups hot broth (1.45 liters)
      or
  10 Tbsps flavor base and 6 cups stock (1.45 liters)
   4 pieces thin deep-fried tofu (abura-age or usu-age)
$2\frac{1}{2}$ Tbsps soy sauce
   1 Tbsp mirin
   1 tsp sugar (optional or season to taste)
   2 leeks
   2 scallions, finely sliced

Make the broth of your choice (pages 43–52).

Boil the tofu for about 2 minutes to remove the excess oil. Discard the water. Add hot water to cover, but not so much that the tofu floats. Turn up the flame and boil for 10 minutes. Again, discard the water.

Add the soy sauce, *mirin*, sugar, and ½ cup (100 cc) broth to the tofu and simmer for about 20 minutes or until the broth is absorbed. While the pieces are hot, open them up, stack them on top of each other, and press down to ensure that they lie flat later. (If you wait until they cool off, they will shrivel up.) Allow to cool, then cut into triangles.

Boil, wash, and reheat the noodles (pages 34–38). Place each portion in its own bowl. Reheat the broth until it begins to boil at the rim, then add the leeks and allow to cook until tender.

Peel the outer skin from the leeks. Cut diagonally into thin slices. Place the leeks and deep-fried tofu triangles on top of the noodles, and cover with the steaming broth. Garnish with the scallion.

Boil the thick tofu (*atsu-age*) for 2 to 3 minutes to remove the excess oil. Puncture the whole outer surface of the tofu with a fork or toothpick.

Put the tofu in a pan and add just enough broth to cover. Add the soy sauce, *mirin*, and sugar and turn the flame up high. As the liquid approaches a boil, turn down the heat and simmer for 20 minutes. As the broth goes down, shake the pan occasionally so that it will be evenly absorbed. Remove from the stove and cut into triangles. Serve as above.

Hot Soba Noodles with Egg Royale
Kakitama Soba

This soba dish features a soft pudding-like thickened broth obtained by thickening the broth with either potato or *kuzu* starch just before stirring in the lightly whipped eggs.

There are several other equally popular egg dishes. *Toji Soba* calls for well-whipped eggs to be added instead of the starch just as the broth comes to a boil. Moonviewing Soba, or *Tsukimi Soba*, dispenses with a thickening agent altogether. Rather, a raw egg is nestled in the center of the noodles and boiling soup broth is poured over it, softly poaching the egg and creating the thin, misty surface which gives it its name.

Serves 3–4

1¼ lbs homemade soba noodles (480–600 g)
   or
1 lb dried soba noodles (450 g)
6 cups hot broth (1.45 liters)
   or
10 Tbsps flavor base and 6 cups stock (1.45 liters)

1   bunch spinach
4   eggs
2   heaping Tbsps potato starch (katakuriko) or kuzu
    or
2   Tbsps cornstarch
4   slices fish cake (kamaboko) (optional)
    2-inch piece ginger, grated
2–3   scallions, finely sliced
4   shiso leaves, chopped (optional)

Make the broth of your choice (pages 43–52).

Cook the spinach and place it in cold water to preserve the color.

Boil and wash the noodles (pages 34–38). While waiting for the water to boil, combine the starch with enough water (about ¼ cup) to achieve a gravy-like texture. Stir until the texture is smooth and all of the lumps dissolve. In a separate bowl, lightly whip the eggs together.

Heat the broth over a high flame. When it begins to boil at the rim, stir the potato starch mixture once again (the starch is prone to collect on the bottom) and then begin to stir the soup broth. When the broth approaches a boil in earnest, add the starch and stir continuously.

A few cautions: If the broth is not sufficiently near the boiling point, it will easily become cloudy when the starch is added. Second, though you are seeking to thicken the broth, you are not after a condensed gelatin texture, but more of a thin gravy effect. The Japanese starch will continue to thicken after it has been added, so make adjustments as necessary. (After several attempts, you will know how you want your broth and the timing needed to achieve this desired result.) Lastly, the heat should be on high or medium-high (depending on the strength of the range) because as you add the starch, the temperature of the broth will drop considerably.

After you have added all of the starch, pour in the egg in a circular motion, beginning at the center and gradually working toward the rim. Knock the handle of the pot 3 or 4 times to ensure a thorough blending, as well as to prevent the starch from sticking to the bottom, then turn off the flame.

Reheat the noodles by putting then in a strainer and dipping them into the hot cooking water. Wring out the spinach and cut into 2-inch (5-cm) lengths. Place the noodles in individual bowls. Pour in the broth, then place the cut spinach and fish cakes on top. Garnish with a dab of ginger, finely sliced scallions, and *shiso*. Serve immediately.

Chicken and Leek Soba

This is a variation of a dish which originally called for duck. Chicken has a lighter taste, is available the year around, and is much cheaper than duck. The aim in cooking the chicken is to maintain a suitably soft and moist texture.

Serves 3–4

1¼ lbs homemade soba noodles (480–600 g)
    or
 1 lb dried soba noodles (450 g)
 6 cups hot broth (1.45 liters)
    or
10 Tbsps flavor base and 6 cups stock (1.45 liters)
 8 oz young chicken (220 g)
 2 leeks
 2 Tbsps soy sauce
 2 Tbsps mirin
 1 tsp sugar (optional)
    Seven-spice pepper (shichimi)

Make the broth of your choice (pages 43–52).

Cut the chicken into thin, bite-sized pieces and the leeks into long, thin, diagonal slices. Fry together in a skillet with the soy sauce, *mirin*, and sugar over high heat for 30–45 seconds.

Boil, wash, and reheat the noodles (pages 34–38).

Place in a bowl, add the chicken and leeks, and cover with the steaming broth. Serve immediately. Season to taste with pepper.

Curry Soba

The hot and spicy taste of curry also complements soba noodles very well. This is one of those dishes that is received equally well in the cold of winter or on a hot summer day. In winter it warms the body, while in the summertime its thick, spicy broth has a cooling and settling effect on the body. Some recipes call for pork, chicken, or shrimp to be added for additional flavor, but curry spice and juicy leeks by themselves produce a sufficiently satisfying dish and the combination is thus quite popular among vegetarians.

Serves 4

1¼   lbs homemade soba noodles (480–600 g)
     or
1   lb dried soba noodles (450 g)
6   cups hot broth (1.45 liters)
     or
10   Tbsps flavor base and 6 cups stock (1.45 liters)
4   tsps curry powder
4   Tbsps potato starch (katakuriko) or kuzu
     or
6   Tbsps cornstarch (or to taste)
2   leeks
2   scallions, finely sliced

Make the broth of your choice (pages 43–52).

Combine the curry and starch with 6 Tbsps broth. Mix well. Chop the leeks in half lengthwise and then into bite-sized pieces so that they will cook easily.

Bring the broth to a boil and add the leeks. Return to a boil, then slowly pour in the curry mixture, stirring constantly. When the broth is adequately thickened, and again comes to a boil, turn off the flame. The strength of the curry and the thickness of the soup is up to your own discretion, but generally a rich gravy-like (but not lumpy) broth with a good, strong curry flavor is the most popular.

Boil, wash, and reheat the noodles (pages 34–38).

Place the noodles in individual bowls. Pour or ladle the broth on top. The broth should amply cover the noodles. Garnish with scallions and serve immediately.

Flavored Soba Noodles
Gozen Soba

Three hundred years ago, soba noodles appealed mainly to priests, temple patrons, country people, laborers, and the lower classes. Soba was cheap and quick to eat, light in calories, yet fortifying and satisfying.

Soba chefs knew they had a good thing. Eventually, they developed a pride in their trade that has carried on down to the present day. Like the sushi or tofu maker, they tried to upgrade their fare by coming up with a more "sophisticated" variation that would appeal to aristocrats, lords, and ultimately the shogun himself. The result was the simple but elegant variation which became known as soba that was fit "to be served before nobles," as the Japanese name implies.

Flavored Soba uses a highly refined, white buckwheat flour. The resulting noodle, with its light taste and texture as well as its appealing snow-white color, is said to have been just the ticket to awaken the upper classes' appreciation of buckwheat. And as its taste is subtly bitter-sweet, it is usually accompanied by only a small amount of broth.

In addition, because this flour is derived from the heart of the kernel it is high in "good quality" starch but low in protein and must be kneaded together with boiling water and wheat flour.

One of the most famous of these noodles is Green Tea Soba. It originated in Shizuoka, an area renowned for its high-quality green tea and the chosen retirement area of the shogun Tokugawa Ieyasu. The leaves of the tea plant are dried and turned into powder. Later, they are mixed into the white buckwheat flour, producing a sweet and aromatic noodle. Some chefs cover the noodles with hot water just before serving them to accentuate the fragrance further.

Serves 4–6

5¼ cups white buckwheat flour (sarashina)* (700 g) and 2¼ cups wheat flour (300 g)
or
4 cups standard buckwheat flour (600 g) and 3 cups wheat flour (400 g)
1¾ cups dipping sauce (420 cc)
or
3¾ Tbsps flavor base and 1¼ cups stock (300 cc)

FLAVORING (choose one)
6 whole yuzu citrus (yellow)
4 oz black sesame seed (black) (110 g)
½ oz parsley or powdered green tea (matcha) (14 g) or 3½ oz shiso leaves (green) (100 g)

Prepare the flavoring first.

YELLOW: Grate the *yuzu* to obtain the zest. Stop before you reach the bitter pith.

BLACK: Grind with a mortar and pestle.

GREEN: Wash the parsley or *shiso* leaves well and then mince or whir in a food processor. The powdered tea can be used as is.

Bring 3 cups (720 cc) water to a boil, put the white buckwheat flour (only!) in a mixing bowl. Make an open hole in the center of the flour, and pour the boiling water in all at once.

Briskly stir the boiling water into the dough with 2–3 long wooden spoons, cooking chopsticks, or pastry whippers. After the first minute of stirring, add the wheat flavoring agent to cold water and knead together.

Continue kneading the dough with your fingertips and palms, as for regular soba (pages 20–33), for at least 2–3 minutes.

Roll out and cut just as for standard soba.

Cook until the noodles are *al dente* (pages 34–38).

*This first combination of flours produces a white noodle if flavoring is omitted. The standard flour produces, of course, the typical brown soba noodle. When adding a flavor to the latter, the colors will be somewhat muted by this darker flour. In Japan, the pure-white *sarashina* flour is a bit more expensive.

Soba Salad

This is a very popular dish to help ward off the summer heat, which may ruin even the heartiest of appetites. The key to this recipe is to prepare a good seasoning and to attain an appetizing balance of colors.

Serves 3–4

1¼	lbs homemade soba noodle (480–600g)	
	or	
1	lb dried soba noodles (450 g)	
1⅛	cups chilled broth (270 cc)	
12	stalks asparagus	
¼	red onion	
1	cucumber	
2	tomatoes	
4	leaves lettuce	
4	oz ham (optional), sliced finely (110 g)	
4	tsps mayonnaise	
4	tsps French dressing	

Make the broth of your choice (pages 43–52) and chill (page 49).

Trim the asparagus and boil for 3 to 4 minutes over a high flame in lightly salted water. Remove from heat to a bowl of cold water.

Slice the onion. Wash and peel the cucumber (if necessary), then quarter lengthwise and cut into bite-sized chunks. Wash the lettuce and tear into small pieces. Slice each tomato into 8 wedges. Dice the ham. Cut the asparagus into 2-inch lengths.

Boil, wash, and drain the noodles (pages 34–38).

Line individual bowls with the lettuce. Add the noodles and garnish with vegetables. Pour in the broth and add a dollop of mayonnaise and French dressing. Mix well before eating.

Front to back: Soba Dumpling with Miso Sauce, Soba Sushi, Soba-Sesame Tofu, Kasha with Mixed Vegetables, Mixed-fry Tempura in a Soba Broth (*nuki*), Soba Noodles, Toasted Nori Seaweed (dusted with buckwheat flour)

Country Cooking

J ust as many parts of Japan have long been famous for their production of high-quality buckwheat, many areas have developed their own distinctive ways of making soba noodles that are likewise famous throughout the country. In fact, having ready access to good-quality buckwheat flour, the people of these areas have grown up appreciating food made from the freshest flour.

Becoming intimate with buckwheat's true character, they naturally developed styles reflecting their understanding. These regional styles enjoy unfading popularity and are appreciated for presenting buckwheat's character in subtly different ways.

A good number of these styles have found their way into the mainstream of soba cuisine, and so properly belong with the general noodle dishes of the preceding section. Two such dishes are Green Tea Soba (page 80) and Cold Soba Noodles with Grated Radish (page 57).

Of the four recipes introduced here, only *Tsugaru Soba* has inherited the name of its place of origin. Other types or variations include *Izumo Soba* (from Shimane Prefecture), *Echizen Soba* (Fukui Prefecture), *Iya Soba* (Tokushima Prefecture), *Tsushima Soba* (Nagasaki Prefecture), *Tokosei Soba* (Hyogo Prefecture), and *Shirakawa Soba* (Fukushima Prefecture). Most or all of

Wanko Soba Party with Tempura

these are either variations on a standard soba recipe or call for the introduction of a favored local food.

"Silk-Cut" Soba takes its name not from a place but rather from the special cutting technique developed to accommodate 100-percent soba noodles. The knife slides across the well-kneaded dough, "shearing" it in the same way as kimono-makers of old sheared high-quality silk.

Of the remaining two recipes, one takes its name from its ingredients, and the other from its container. Soba Noodles in a Miso Stew received its Japanese name from the smorgasbord of ingredients added to the miso soup. Wanko Soba got its from the small bowls automatically replenished with further portions of noodles until the diner called a stop. This all-you-can-eat style originated in real soba country.

Soba Noodles in a Miso Stew
Kenchin Soba (Ibaraki Prefecture)

Ibaraki Prefecture lies to the north of Tokyo and is known for its tasty produce, such as carrots, burdock, and daikon radishes. This dish combines tender vegetables sautéed in sesame oil with soba and a miso broth for a hearty bowl of noodles, said to have been eaten in earlier times by the famed samurai of Mito (a clan related to the Tokugawa) at New Year to ensure strength and vigor.

Today, local residents turn to this stew-like soba dish for warmth and nourishment when they need to fend off the cold of winter. The blend of miso and broth is sure to satisfy Western palates as well, be they those of warriors or not.

THE BOOK OF SOBA

1¼	lbs fresh noodles (480–600 g)	**Serves 4**
	or	
1	lb dried noodles (450 g)	
7	Tbsps flavor base	
6	cups stock (1.45 liters)	
½	block tofu	
1	burdock root	
1	carrot	
2	oz bamboo shoot (60 g)	
4	dried shiitake mushrooms, soft-ened (page 133)	
6	leaves spinach	
¼	lb chicken (optional) (115 g)	
2	Tbsps sesame or vegetable oil	
4–5	Tbsps miso	
	Pinch salt	
	Dash saké	

Cut the tofu into 6 or 8 pieces, wrap in cellophane, and freeze overnight. Thaw and squeeze out the moisture.

Combine the stock and flavor base.

Sliver the burdock and carrots and soak the burdock in water. Slice the bamboo shoots diagonally. Slice the mushrooms.

Parboil the spinach and place in a bowl of cold water (to maintain the color). Wring out and cut into 2-inch lengths.

Cut the chicken into small pieces, season well with salt and saké, and pan-fry in oil. In a separate pan, lightly sauté the burdock and carrots.

Place the vegetables, chicken, and tofu in the stock and allow to boil for just a moment. Dissolve the miso in ½ cup of hot broth. Add to broth, stir well, and remove from heat.

Boil, wash, and reheat the noodles (pages 34–38), then place in serving bowls. Cover with the broth and serve immediately.

VARIATION: Serve the hot broth as a dipping sauce with chilled noodles.

Soy-Soba Noodles

Tsugaru Soba (Aomori Prefecture)

This style was very popular at the "nighthawk" soba carts in eighteenth- and nineteenth-century Tokyo. By substituting mashed soybeans for water during the all-important mixing process, the soba masters of old found that they could not only offer a new, flavorful noodle but could also keep the cooked noodles for as long as 3 or 4 days. (Standard noodles are prone to dry and turn sour within 12 to 24 hours, depending on the season.) The ability of this soy-soba noodle to maintain its freshness led to the nickname "illusion soba." That is, if properly wrapped and stored, the noodles look as fresh three or four days later as they do on the day they are made.

4 oz soybeans (115 g)	**Serves 4**
½ cup water (120 cc)	
4 cups buckwheat flour (540 g)	
2 cups wheat flour (270 g)	

DAY ONE

Soak the soybeans in ample water until they double in size. In warm summer weather this will take 10 to 12 hours. In winter, allow 24 hours.

Bring ¼ cup (60 cc) of water to a boil and remove from heat. Add ¾ cup (100 g) of buckwheat flour and mix following the recipe for Soba Dumpling (page 103).

Remove dough to a large bowl of cold water (use ice water in hot weather). Let sit overnight.

DAY TWO

Rinse and wash the soybeans. Slowly grind with a mortar and pestle or whir in a food processor until you achieve a smooth, porridge-like consistency (add a small amount of water if necessary).

Drain the dumpling dough and mix together with the remaining buckwheat and wheat flours.

Now, adding only about one-third of the soybean puree at a time, mix together following the directions in Homemade Soba Noodles (page 21). No additional water is necessary.

Roll out the noodles and cut.

Set aside for least 5 hours in summer and overnight in winter until the noodles turn an amber or light brown and their fragrance is irresistible.

Cook as you would regular soba noodles (pages 34–38). Serve immediately.

Wanko Soba

(Iwate Prefecture)

In the Tohoku district of northern Japan, this soba has been served for several centuries. Today, travelers to the area always seek out this regional fare, perfect for hearty appetites.

The "spirit of *wanko*" (which means "small bowl") is akin to that of all-you-can-eat buffets in the West. Traditionally, contests have been held to determine a local champion. A waiter or waitress stands behind each contestant, replacing the petite bowls of noodles as fast as they are emptied. A mouthwatering assortment of condiments—mushrooms, cooked greens, sashimi, shrimp, and so on—is served along with the noodles, and hungry contestants have been known to eat upward of 50 or 60 bowls of fresh soba pasta!

Wanko's legacy pervades the area. Even out-of-town customers who stop in at a local soba shop are asked—with a smile—if they would like to try to best the existing shop record.

In any case, this style of soba lends itself to picnics,

parties, or any buffet-type affair—all the more so since soba and alcohol go well together.

The toppings below are only suggestions. Add to them or change the portions as you see fit. Other possible toppings may include cooked and chopped greens (such as spinach or asparagus), ground chicken, or cottage cheese and pineapple.

Serves 6–8

2½ lbs fresh soba noodles (1–1.2 kilograms)
   or
1½ lbs dried soba noodles (600 g)
2 cups flavor base (480 cc)
6 cups stock (1.45 liters)
1 lb assorted seafood (cooked shrimp or white fish; sushi toppings such as tuna sashimi, shrimp, salmon roe, etc.) (450 g)
   Dash saké (for salmon roe)
   Oil for deep-frying (for tempura)
½ lb cooked greens (spinach, asparagus, cabbage, etc.) (225 g)

CONDIMENTS

8 Tbsps sesame seeds (120g)
1 cup sliced scallion (200 g)
1 cup grated daikon radish (200 g)
1–2 sheets nori seaweed, toasted (page 131) and shredded
   Bonito flakes

Combine flavor base and stock to make broth. Set aside to cool for about 2 hours or force-cool in a large bowl of ice water.

Roast the sesame seeds in a dry skillet until they begin to emit a nice nut-like fragrance. Do not allow them to pop. Remove them immediately from the pan. Serve whole or grind into a coarse powder.

To ensure their maximum freshness, prepare the daikon and onions just before serving. If prepared earlier, wrap tightly in plastic wrap.

Prepare the seafood. If you are using shrimp, boil them (seasoning to taste) or make tempura (page 58). Season salmon roe with a dash of saké. Deep-fry white fish and chop into bite-sized pieces. Lastly, coarsely chop tuna or other sashimi.

Chop cooked greens into bite-sized pieces.

Arrange each topping neatly in its own dish. Since there are a variety of toppings, try to use dishes of the same color and size. Place a folded white napkin under oily foods.

Cook the noodles and cool (pages 34–38) just before you are ready to sit down at the table.

Serve the noodles at room temperature. Set them out on a large platter and allow the diners to help themselves. Take a small portion of noodles and cover it with one or more toppings. Dip the noodles halfway into the chilled sauce. Season the dipping sauce with one or more condiments of your choice.

"Silk Cut" Soba
Tachi Soba (Fukushima Prefecture)

There are three technical feats about this style that make it stand out from the rest. One is that the dough is made with 100-percent buckwheat flour. Second, boiling water is added to start the kneading process and then, after about 1 minute of kneading, cold water is introduced.

Third, a unique cutting method is employed which closely resembles the cutting of silk for a kimono. The Japanese verb *tatsu* refers to pulling the cutting knife straight down and through the material. Hence, this style has become known as *Tachi Soba*. (It should not be confused, however, with *tachi-gui*, the "instant" variety of soba found at fast-food soba stands.)

One place where *Tachi Soba* is recorded to have originated is in the remote mountain village of Hinoemata in Fukushima Prefecture, where snow covers the ground during half of the year. Buckwheat was one of the only crops that flourished, and other staples such as wheat and rice were simply not obtainable. As a result, the people developed this unique style, which allowed them to make 100-percent buckwheat noodles.

These noodles were accompanied by only the simplest of broths (again, due to limited local food sources), and when the supply of soy sauce ran out, homemade miso was used to liven up the soup. Fish from the cold mountain stream that divides Hinoemata were also used to make a broth. Fortunately, today there are more choices. Choose any of the broths in this book or whip up a hearty one of your own.

Serves 8–10

3   cups fresh, high-quality buckwheat flour (400 g)
    (or use 2 cups buckwheat flour and 1 cup wheat
    flour)
2   cups water (480 cc)

Add ³⁄₄ cup (180 cc) boiling water to the buckwheat flour. Knead for 45–60 seconds and then add 1¹⁄₄ cups (300 cc) cold water. Knead the dough thoroughly as in Homemade Soba Noodles (pages 20–33) and then divide it into 4 or 5 balls.

With a standard rolling pin, roll out each ball separately until it attains a nice circular shape with a thickness of $\frac{1}{8}$ inch (3 mm). Roll away from the body, turning the dough like a steering wheel, with your hands at 10 and 2, after every 3 or 4 rolls. Stack one piece on top of the other, lightly sprinkling with flour to prevent sticking.

Cut the stack in half and place one pile on the other. This helps somewhat to prevent the dough from tearing when you cut. (Do not fold the dough. It will crack and tear easily because it contains little or no wheat, so lacks gluten to bind the dough.)

Now you are ready for the "silk cutting." Place your left hand on the dough with your left thumb near the cut edge. Align the knife with the edge so that your thumb is alongside the blade. Slide your hand 1 to 2 inches toward you, then cut into the dough with the knife, pulling it almost to your thumb. Repeat this slide-cut movement to cut a noodle $\frac{1}{8}$ inch wide.

The left hand accompanies and actually leads the slicing motion of the knife. It takes only a few times to get a feel for the rhythm required. Even if you can only approximate a shoelace-type shape, the noodles have a special edge to them that is different from the edges of noodles obtained from the professional's big thick knife. After a few attempts, the cutting becomes easier and easier.

Because this noodle is made from 100-percent buckwheat flour, it dries out easily and must be protected. When finished rolling and cutting, wrap in newspaper or plastic wrap and keep in a cool place to prevent drying, unless you are going to cook and serve the noodles immediately. Noodles keep 2 to 3 days, depending on the weather.

Cook following the standard instructions (pages 34–38), but treat more gently. If they appear as if they may break apart during the cooking, place them in a wire strainer and lower it into slowly boiling water. Cook until done (1 minute), testing frequently. Serve immediately.

Groat Cooking

S erved as a staple food in several parts of Europe, groats are an unpretentious food that provide a nice alternative or addition to any breakfast, lunch, or dinner menu.

In Japan, groats might be served up in a stew along with ingredients such as shiitake mushrooms, bamboo shoots, onions, chicken, and shrimp; dressed with various kinds of sauces as part of the soba haute cuisine (*soba kaiseki*) course; or even included in a miso sauce topping for a soba dumpling. In Russia, groats were formerly eaten by the lower class and nobility alike. In fact, buttered groats was the favorite dish of the czar Peter the Great, and some said that he seldom supped on anything else.

Boiled Groats
Kasha

When cooking groats, remember that the time required will differ according to the amount of water, the variety of the groat, the season, and so on, but about 20 minutes is a good rule of thumb to go by.

Groats are usually boiled, but they are sometimes dry-roasted in a skillet first for added flavor. The boiling method here employs a little-by-little approach. That is, the cooking water is changed twice as soon as it comes to a boil. Only the third pot of cooking water is kept. In this way, the color of the groats becomes lighter, the taste subtler yet, and the tedious process of washing the groats over and over is eliminated. This method of preparation comes from soba haute cuisine.

2   cups groats (270 g)   **Serves 4**

Roast the groats before boiling, if desired. To do this, heat them in a dry skillet over a medium flame until they turn a golden brown and emit a nut-like fragrance. Stir often and do not allow them to scorch.

Wash the groats, put into a pot, and add water to cover. Bring the water to a boil over a medium-high flame.

Drain, return to the pot, add water to cover, and bring to a boil a second time.

Drain the groats and return to the pot a third time. Add 2¼ cups water (540 cc), reduce heat to low and simmer for 15–20 minutes until the water has been absorbed.

Serve plain or seasoned to taste with butter, sour cream, or grated cheese.

Groats Simmered in a Bonito Stock

| 2 | cups groats (270 g) | **Serves 4** |
| 2½ | cups bonito stock (600 cc) | |

Make the stock of your choice (pages 43–52).

Wash and rinse the groats thoroughly. Soak in the stock for 1 hour.

Bring the groats and stock to a boil and then simmer (loosely covered) over a very low heat until the groats become light and fluffy and all the liquid is absorbed (about 30 minutes).

Buckwheat Groats and Brown Rice Mushi
Mushi

Here is a prime example of the complementary proteins and vitamins of separate foods boosting the overall protein value of a dish (as discussed in the Nutrition section).

1⅓	cups brown rice (175 g)	**Serves 4**
⅔	cup buckwheat groats (90 g)	
3	cups water (720 cc)	
4	fresh shiitake mushroom, thinly sliced	
½	lb chicken, sliced (optional) (225 g)	
½	carrot, finely chopped	
6	oz bamboo shoots, finely sliced (180 g)	
1	block tofu, chopped into small cubes	
4	Tbsps flavor base	
	or	
3	Tbsps soy sauce, 1 Tbsp mirin, and 1 tsp sugar	

Wash the brown rice and buckwheat groats well and let sit overnight.

Strain and bring to a boil in 3 cups water. Reduce to a simmer and cook (loosely covered) for 35 to 40 minutes.

After 25 minutes, layer in the remaining ingredients.

Cover with the flavor base and allow to simmer and finish cooking. Serve in bowls.

Groat Salad with Vinegar Dressing

1	cup buckwheat groats (150 g)	**Serves 4**
8	small or 4 large shrimp	
½	oz dry wakame seaweed (14 g)	
1	small cucumber	
2	Tbsps light soy sauce	
4	Tbsps rice vinegar	
2	Tbsps mirin	
2	Tbsps stock	
1	oz walnuts, chopped (28 g)	

Cook the groats as you would for Kasha (page 96).

Clean the shrimp and remove the tail. Boil for 1 minute in lightly salted water.

Soak the *wakame* in water for 15 minutes. Rinse well and chop finely. Slice the cucumber into thin rounds.

Combine the soy sauce, *mirin*, vinegar, and stock.

Lightly toss the groats, shrimp, *wakame*, and cucumber. Cover with the dressing, sprinkle with the walnuts, and serve.

Soba Groat Zosui

Zosui

1	cup buckwheat groats (150 g)	**Serves 4**
1	cup leftover rice	
½	block tofu	
4	leaves spinach, finely chopped	
6	mushrooms, coarsely chopped	
¼	lb ground chicken (115 g)	
¼	carrot, diced	
4	cups hot soba stock (pages 43–52) (960 cc)	

6   Tbsps flavor base (90 cc)
    or
4   Tbsps soy sauce, 1½ Tbsps mirin, and 2 tsps sugar

Wash the groats well and soak in water for about an hour.

Heat up the stock and add the rice and groats when it reaches a boil.

Add the remaining ingredients, lower the flame slightly, and pour in the flavor base. Simmer for 5 to 7 minutes. Serve piping hot in soup bowls.

Groat and Okara Mélange

⅓	cup buckwheat groats (50 g)	**Serves 4**

3–4   Tbsps vegetable oil
½   carrot, diced
2   fresh shiitake or other mushrooms, thinly sliced
8   green beans, slivered
7   oz okara (200 g)
3   Tbsps light soy sauce
2   Tbsps sugar

1   Tbsps mirin
½   cup hot soba stock (pages 43–52) (120 cc)

Soak the groats in water for 2 hours. When they become swollen, drain off the remaining water.

Heat oil in a pan and stir-fry the vegetables and the groats for a few minutes.

Add the *okara*, soy sauce, sugar, and *mirin* and continue stirring for 3 to 4 minutes until the *okara* emits a nut-like fragrance.

Finally, add the stock and cook over a medium flame until the liquid is absorbed (about 5 minutes). Serve in a fluffy mound garnished with a few slivers of cooked green beans.

Seafood Groat Patties

2   cups buckwheat groats (270–300 g)   **Serves 4**
5   cups soba stock (pages 43–52) (1.2 liters)
8   eggs
¼   lb fish, diced (115 g)
6   clams, diced
1   onion, diced
    Garlic to taste

First, cook the groats in the stock following the recipe on page 98. Drain off excess liquid.

Beat the eggs. Mix the fish, clams, onions, and garlic together in a bowl and then combine with the egg.

Finally mix in the very soft and well-cooked groats. Form into thin patties and fry in a skillet until cooked through (about 5 minutes).

Groat and Mountain Yam Fry

<table>
<tr><td>⅓</td><td>cup buckwheat groats (50 g)</td><td>Serves 4</td></tr>
<tr><td></td><td>Rice vinegar (for soaking yam)</td><td></td></tr>
<tr><td>7</td><td>oz mountain yam (yama imo) (200 g)</td><td></td></tr>
<tr><td>1½</td><td>cups bonito stock (pages 43–52) (360 cc)</td><td></td></tr>
<tr><td></td><td>Pinch sugar</td><td></td></tr>
<tr><td></td><td>Pinch salt</td><td></td></tr>
<tr><td>3</td><td>Tbsps potato starch (katakuriko) or cornstarch</td><td></td></tr>
<tr><td></td><td>Oil for deep-frying</td><td></td></tr>
</table>

Wash the groats well and parboil in 1 cup water. Allow to cool.

Peel the yam and soak in vinegar water (5 parts water to 1 part vinegar) for about 5 minutes. Cut into rounds. Bring the stock, sugar, and salt to a boil, add the yams, and simmer until soft (3 to 5 minutes).

Grind the yam and stock with a mortar and pestle. Pour this thickened mixture into the bowl of cooked groats and mix well.

Form into ping-pong-sized balls. Roll in starch.

Preheat the oil. Deep-fry balls until they float and turn a golden brown.

Variations and Desserts

Soba Dumpling
Soba gaki

Though of plain appearance, this dumpling provides the maximum benefits of buckwheat's nutritional elements, notably vitamin B. Furthermore, since all of the water used in the recipe is combined with the flour during the cooking process practically all of buckwheat's water-soluble elements remain in the dumpling itself. (The professional, however, boils the finished dumpling one more time after mixing to create a softer, more delicate texture.)

There are two basic methods of making buckwheat dumplings: in a pot over a flame or in a bowl. The pot method requires a high flame during the beating process to heat the dough, while the bowl style takes the opposite approach of pouring boiling water into the bowl of flour and beating without the benefit of any additional heat. In the pot method, the buckwheat flour can either be combined with cold water before beating over a flame (a good technique for beginners to use), or, after you gain more confidence, the flour can be mixed with rapidly boiling water (the professional method).

The pot style has a higher success rate as the buckwheat flour has virtually no choice but to gelatinize with continuous heating and pounding. Plus, you can adjust

Foreground: Soba Pasty, Saké-seasoned Soba Patties, Soba Mochi Squares. Pit: Stew with Soba Dumplings, Soba Dumplings with Miso Sauce (light and dark flour)

the flame as you go along. Since these factors play no role in the bowl method, be sure to use rapidly boiling water.

There is a delicate difference between immersing flour (buckwheat or any other kind) into a pot of boiling water, and pouring boiling water into a bowl of flour. The pot style provides a smoother, shinier, and more consistent texture. On the other hand, it is claimed that the fragrance of the dumpling obtained by the bowl method is superior: buckwheat's delicate and treasured fragrance has no chance to escape since the flour is not heated or cooked.

This last point provides a useful hint, whichever method is employed. That is, while working to develop buckwheat's viscosity, you must also move quickly so as to prevent any loss of its delicate fragrance.

The pot method is introduced in detail below. Once you become familiar with the way buckwheat behaves under heat you will be able go on to the professional method, or if you prefer you can make the dumpling in a bowl simply by transferring the boiling water to a large mixing bowl.

		Serves 4
$4^{1}/_2$	cups buckwheat flour (600 g)	
$2^{1}/_3$	cups water* (560 cc)	
$1^{3}/_4$	cups chilled broth (420 cc)	
	or	
7	Tbsps flavor base and $1^{1}/_4$ cups stock (300 cc)	
	Nori seaweed, toasted and shredded (page 131)	
	Wasabi horseradish	
1	stalk scallion, finely sliced	

Make the broth of your choice (pages 43–52).

Divide both the flour and water in half. Combine one portion of water with one portion of flour. Mix well.

Over a high flame, beat the flour into the water using a pestle (4 to 5 chopsticks clenched in one fist, a wooden spoon, or even a spatula in emergencies). With quick, rhythmical, circular strokes, begin to combine the flour and the dough. Keep the wrist loose. At this initial stage, the flour and water will not form a dough easily, but will form small, marble-sized pebbles. (Interestingly, this is exactly what happens during the initial stages of soba noodle making: *it takes time for the flour to bind together into one large ball of dough*.)

As you continue beating rhythmically, stroke by stroke, the dough will begin to form. Continue to beat in a circular motion and gather all of the dough into a single ball against the side of the pan closest you. When this is achieved, remove from the heat. (The pros, who are aiming for the highest degree of sweetness, continue beating over a medium-high flame until they can smell a sweet, scorching fragrance, and the surface of the dough closest to the heat turns a light brown similar to that of crepes.)

Lay a slightly moist cloth or towel on top of the counter. Place the pot on the towel and continue beating until you achieve a smooth, gelatinized texture. (Although it contains no gluten, buckwheat does have a large amount of high-quality starch which becomes extremely sticky and viscous when mixed with hot water.) Keep in mind that the whole beating process takes only 40 to 60 seconds and that the movement of the pestle will meet with increasing resistance as the gelatinization occurs.

As the dough forms and the pestle becomes more difficult to wield, a pleasant "puckering" sound will become audible. This is your assurance that you have performed the job well. There should be a distinct difference in the texture of the dough before and after you hear this sound. Continue beating for another 5 seconds to achieve a firm dough.

Switching from the pestle to a flat wooden spoon or rice paddle (any flat-surfaced utensil will do), press the finished soba dumpling into a nicely compact shape against the side of the pot. Dip the paddle in hot water 2 or 3 times during this final stage to obtain a smoother and shinier surface. Divide into 2 balls. Decorate the tops with a simple design. (Professionals use the edge of their wood paddle to incise a leaf pattern.)

Repeat the process with the remaining flour.

Serve with heated or chilled broth. Garnish with the *nori*, *wasabi*, and scallion.

*According to the time of year and condition of the flour, the amount of water required can vary by as much as 20 percent. Freshly harvested flour needs less water than flour that has been sitting on the shelf. Furthermore, the quality of the grind will also influence the moisture content of the flour.

The key to success in almost all of the buckwheat recipes lies in adding the water quickly but little by little. Stop just before you think you have enough. After 5 or 10 attempts, you will develop a good intuitive sense as to how much water to add.

Steamed Soba Dumpling with Shrimp and Mountain Yam

3	cups buckwheat flour (400 g)	**Serves 4**
1½	cups dipping sauce (360 cc)	
	or	
¼	cup flavor base (60 cc) and 1¼ cups cold stock (300 cc)	
1¼	cups hot stock (300 cc)	
1	avocado	
5	oz shrimp (140 g)	
5	oz mountain yam (yama imo) (140 g)	

Make the broth and stock of your choice (pages 43–52) and let cool.

Scoop out the fruit of the avocado and grind in a mortar. Stir in the dipping sauce and blend into a creamy sauce.

Shell and devein the shrimp. With the dull back side of a heavy cooking knife, beat the shrimp into a pulp.

Peel the yam. Grate into a mortar. Add shrimp and 1 Tbsp of stock. Grind with a pestle until it becomes smooth.

Combine this mixture with the buckwheat flour and half of the stock. Knead the dough following the directions for Soba Dumpling (page 103). Add broth as necessary. Form into small patties.

Cook the dumplings in a preheated steamer for 4 to 5 minutes, or until little bubble pockets form like beads on the outside. Serve with the avocado dipping sauce.

VARIATION: Substitute walnuts, *shiso*, and egg yolks for the yam. Place 1 oz walnuts, 1⅔ oz (18 g) *shiso* leaves, and 2 egg yolks in a food processor or blender. Whip well and then combine with flour and stock.

Broiled Soba Dumplings with Miso Sauce

These savory miso-covered dumplings are best eaten "hot off the grill." The fragrant *yuzu* peel (which is also used in Korean and Chinese cooking) imparts a unique zestfulness to the miso sauce, but if it is not readily available lemon or lime may be substituted.

Serves 4

4½	cups buckwheat flour (600 g)
2¼	cups water (540 cc)
3–4	Tbsps sweet white miso (45–60 g)
1	Tbsp grated *yuzu* zest (or lemon or lime zest)
1	tsp sugar or 1 Tbsp amazake
2	tsps basil
	Skewers (optional)

Make the soba dumplings (page 103) and shape into hamburger-sized patties.

Make the miso sauce by mixing the miso with a little lukewarm water. Add the grated *yuzu* and mix well, then add the sugar.

Pierce with skewers. Hold over a medium-low flame and turn over and over to scorch both sides lightly (or set the patties on a tray and place in a broiler).

Brush with a liberal coating of miso sauce, sprinkle with basil to taste, and pass over a flame (or broil) for about 30 to 40 seconds. Serve immediately.

Soba-Sesame Tofu

Serves 4

1½	cups buckwheat flour (dark flour is best) (200 g)
3	oz sesame butter or tahini (84 g)
1½	oz kuzu starch (42 g).
2	cups cold water (480 cc)
1	scallion, finely sliced
	Soy sauce
	Wasabi *horseradish*

Dissolve the starch in the cold water and allow it to sit for a moment. Stir well until the starch is completely dissolved. Run your fingertips along the bottom to make sure there are no hard clumps. (To obtain a softer texture, slightly decrease the amount of *kuzu*.) Add buckwheat flour and stir well.

Put the sesame butter into pot. Heat over a medium flame stirring constantly with a wooden *surikogi* for 2 to 3 minutes. Remove from the stove. When the mixture starts to harden beat down like pounding *mochi* while holding the pot firmly. After about 30 seconds of intense pounding, the texture should combine completely and lift easily out of the pot in one gelatinous ball. Transfer the mixture into a pie or bread pan and refrigerate for 5 to 6 hours.

Before serving garnish with the scallion, soy sauce, and *wasabi*. The recommended ingredients should produce a fairly firm and grainy tofu texture.

Soba Sushi Roll

The thought of making sushi with soba noodles instead of rice always seems to raise eyebrows. Part of the reason is that rice is so closely associated with sushi. People also can't imagine how the long, slender noodles could possibly be tightly rolled into the required form. Yet once they get the hang of it, the idea that sushi belongs exclusively to the domain of rice quickly changes.

There are four key points for making good Soba Sushi:

1. Undercook the noodles slightly, cutting the cooking time by 10 to 15 seconds. (Aim: To produce a noodle that is cooked sufficiently, but just shy of attaining its fully elasticity.)

2. Wash and rinse the noodles thoroughly in cold water, or ice water in summer. (Aim: To firm up the noodle

Front to back: Soba Sushi, Soba-Sesame Tofu, Soba Crepe

and keep it fresh. Later, this will provide the sushi with a nice chewy quality.)

3. Thoroughly drain the water from the noodles. (Aim: To prevent the noodles from becoming soggy.)

4. Work as quickly as possible. (Aim: To ensure the above three conditions.)

Just as with sushi rice, the soba noodles can be seasoned with rice vinegar, broth, or other flavoring agents. This recipe, however, will introduce a simple, unseasoned sushi.

2¼	lbs cooked soba noodles (1 kg)	**Yields 8 rolls**
8	sheets nori *seaweed*	
5–6	fresh shiitake or other mushrooms	
3	oz bamboo shoots (80 g)	
6	Tbsps soy sauce	
2	Tbsps mirin	
2	tsps sugar	
3	oz tuna (84 g)	
¼	cup finely sliced scallions	
4	eggs	
2	tsps sugar	
¼	cup hot soba broth (pages 43–52), cooled	
⅔	oz shiso leaves (20 g)	
1½	oz cucumber (40 g)	
3	oz cod roe tarako or any sashimi (80 g)	
3	oz salmon roe (ikura), sprinkled with dash saké (80 g)	
	Soy sauce	
	Wasabi *horseradish*	
	Bamboo rolling mat	
	Cheesecloth	

Trim the width of the *nori* by one inch with a pair of scissors.

Wash the mushrooms and bamboo, then slice very thinly. Combine each vegetable in its own pot with 3 Tbsps soy sauce, 1 Tbsp *mirin*, 1 tsp sugar, and enough water to cover. Bring to a boil, then simmer, loosely covered, until all of the liquid is absorbed (about 30 minutes).

Mix the tuna and scallion and then beat together with the dull side of a heavy knife.

Beat the eggs, cooled broth, and 2 tsps sugar together and cook as in "Rosy-Cheeked" Soba (page 69). Remove from the pan and set on a plate to cool. Repeat with the rest of the mixture. Cut each batch lengthwise into 3- or $4^1/_2$-inch-wide strips.

Cut the *shiso* leaves into thin, $^1/_8$-inch-wide strips.

Wash the cucumber and then slice it and the sashimi into long, slender strips.

Cook the noodles (pages 34–38), keeping the four key points in mind. Wash them in cold water as soon as they are done.

You cannot relax yet. If the noodles are left sitting in the rinsing bowl too long, they will absorb too much water before you know it. So the next step is quickly to shift the washed noodles to a large, dry strainer (or plate covered with cheesecloth). To prevent clumps or improper drying, the noodles should be spread around the edges of the strainer 4 to 5 strands at a time. Since the sides of the strainer slope inward, the water will naturally be inclined to flow in that direction, away from the noodles.

Allow to sit for 4–5 minutes. Fan with a newspaper. (You could add vinegar to the process at this point, if so desired.)

Remove the noodles to a second dry strainer (or plate with cheesecloth) and allow to dry for an additional 4 to 5 minutes, fanning occasionally.

MAKING THE SUSHI ROLLS

Place a piece of cellophane over the bamboo rolling mat and on top of that place 1 sheet of *nori*. Spread out 20 to 25 noodles on the *nori*, leaving a 1-inch strip of *nori* uncovered at both the near and far ends.

Next place a long strip of egg in the middle of the noodles and on top of that, a few strips of *shiso*. To ensure that the egg and *shiso* stay in place, cover with another small mound of about 5 or 6 noodles.

Take hold of the end of the bamboo roller closest to you, and in one decisive motion, fold over to the point just past the furthest edge of the egg and *shiso*. Press down gently and hold for 3 seconds. Then with "the feeling of walking lightly with your fingers," roll forward until you reach the uncovered strip of *nori* at the far end. Again push down and hold. Finally, roll forward to cover the last bit of *nori* and again press and hold. With practice you should be able to make a clean, firm, and beautifully shaped roll. If you succeed the first time, consider opening your own restaurant. You have talent.

Proceed to wrap remaining ingredients in the following combinations: mushroom with bamboo shoot, cucumber with cod roe (or sashimi), and salmon roe alone (to top the sushi after it has been cut). (By the way, the combinations of stuffing for Soba Sushi are limitless. Anything that you can make into a soft yet firm shape will work well.)

Since the rolls should be cut just before serving, keep wrapped in the cellophane and put in a cool place (but not in the refrigerator). When ready to cut, unwrap and place a damp cloth close by. Wipe both sides of a sharp knife on the towel and cut a $1\frac{1}{2}$-inch piece off in one smooth, continuous motion. Once you begin the slicing motion, do not stop until you have cut completely through the roll. Clean the knife on the cloth and make a second cut. Repeat until you have cut all the rolls.

NOTE: To make individual pieces of soba sushi with standard sushi toppings such as shrimp or squid (see color plate), simply press the noodles into a long block with a rolling mat lined with plastic wrap, cut into 2-inch lengths, and cover with the topping of your choice.

Soba Pasty

This recipe allows you to show your creativity. The buckwheat dough can be stuffed with either sweet foods such as homemade pie or fruit filling, or sandwich-type fare such as hamburger, meat, cheese, or vegetables. Choose either of the fillings below or try one of your own.

4	cups buckwheat flour (540 g)	**Serves 4**
2¼	cups boiling water (225 cc)	

FILLINGS

    1½   oz natto (40 g)

    4   tsps ground sesame seed

    ½   lb pickled vegetables (tsukemono) or parboiled spinach (225 g)

       or

    ½   lb fresh berries, peaches, or any other soft fruit (225 g)

    4   Tbsps sugar

Chop the *natto* as you would for Natto Soba (page 66). Mince the pickled vegetables or spinach (drain well first). Sprinkle with the sesame and mash together with the dull side of a knife. Season with soy sauce.

Chop the fruit. Parboil and drain well.

Combine the dough and water as for Soba Dumpling (page 103).

Divide the dough into 4 portions. Knead 1 of the balls separately in the mixing bowl about 10 times, take it out of the bowl, and knead with both hands to re-form into a ball. Keep a bowl of cold water on hand to moisten your hands as necessary.

Holding a ball of dough in the palm of the left hand, make a hole in the center of the ball with the index finger of your right hand. Rotate the ball, gradually widening the hole with your middle, index, and fifth fingers until you have formed the dough into a cup about the size of a half grapefruit. Use your fingers and finally a fist to shape the dough.

Pack in a tablespoon of filling at a time and gently press it down. Stop $\frac{1}{2}$ inch shy of the rim. For the fruit filling, spoon 1 Tbsp sugar into each cup.

Still holding the cup in the left palm, turn it around and around, gradually pinching the edges toward the center to close off the opening. Moisten your hands as often as necessary.

Steam or bake until small bubbles start to form on the surface. Serve immediately.

Soba Crepe

Buckwheat crepes have been a traditional dish in France for centuries. A French restaurant in Tokyo, where I once helped out for two weeks, made soba crepes for the dinner menu. Choose one of the three fillings below, or stuff the crepes with a dinner or desert filling of your own.

Makes 4 crepes

1	cup buckwheat flour (140 g)
1½	tsp salt
1	egg
1½	cups water (360 cc)
	Zest from 2 lemons, diced
	Butter

FILLINGS (choose one)

¼	lb chicken (115 g)
½	cup hot soba broth (pages 43–52) (50 cc)
1	tsp yuzu or lemon zest
4	tsps mustard

or

16	strips bacon
4	oz cheese (112 g)
4	eggs

or

1	bundle asparagus
3	oz mushrooms (80 g)
1⅓	cups milk (130 cc)
⅔	cup cream (65 cc)
¼	cup wheat flour (35 g)
1	tsp oregano
2	tsps salt

Prepare the filling of your choice.

CHICKEN: Slice the chicken into 8 thin pieces, spread out 4 pieces each on a piece of tinfoil, fold up all the sides to make a tray, and pour in $1/4$ cup of hot broth. Sprinkle on the *yuzu* zest, fold up foil, and put in a pot. Turn the flame up high and boil for 1 minute. Take out and cut each piece in half.

BACON: Fry the bacon and grate the cheese.

VEGETABLE: Boil the asparagus and mushrooms for 1 minute. Slice the mushrooms. Bring the milk, cream, wheat flour, oregano, and salt to a boil, then add the asparagus and mushrooms and simmer for 20 minutes.

Put the buckwheat flour and salt in a bowl and mix well. In a separate bowl, combine the lemon zest, water, and egg and beat well. Add to the flour and beat the mixture until it becomes even and creamy. Put into a bowl, cover with plastic wrap, and place in the refrigerator for at least an hour. (Professionals let it sit overnight.)

To cook the crepe, coat a saucepan with ample butter. (Try to use a pan that has been broken in, in order to avoid sticking.) Melt the butter over a high flame and pour off the excess.

Lower the heat to medium-low, add another dab of butter and melt. Ladle in some batter. It should sizzle softly. Spread the batter by tilting the pan.

Fry the crepe until the batter just sets, then flip over. Add the fillings in layers.

For the chicken, spread the mustard first, the lettuce second, and the chicken third. For the bacon, first spread a layer of cheese, then the bacon, and finally crack open an egg on top. For the vegetables, ladle some of the thickened sauce directly on the crepe, then add the asparagus and mushroom.

As soon as the fillings have been added fold up the crepe. Fold up the top and bottom, then fold in the sides. Make sure the crepe covers the fillings completely, so that it will seal. Cook until the crepe turns a light brown, then flip over and finish cooking.

Cover with melted butter or a sauce of your choice and serve immediately.

Deep-fried Cinnamon Soba Dumpling with Tartar Sauce

4½	cups buckwheat flour (600 g)	**Serves 4**
⅓	cup raisins, chopped (40 g)	
2	Tbsps ground cinnamon	
1	tsp salt	
2⅓	cups hot soba broth (pages 43–52) (560 cc)	
	Oil for deep-frying	
	Tartar sauce	

Combine the raisins, cinnamon, and salt with the buckwheat flour.

Bring half of the broth to a boil, mix in half of the flour mixture, and beat into a dough following the standard Soba Dumpling method (page 103). Form into thin hamburger-shaped patties.

Preheat the oil to a low deep-frying temperature (300°–330°F/150°–165°C). Deep-fry the dumplings until they float (about 1 minute).

Cover with Tartar sauce and serve immediately.

Sweet Soba "Marshmallow" Dumplings
Soba Dango

As this recipe calls for a seemingly preposterous amount of sugar, it will probably cause surprise among the health-food crowd. But the fact of the matter is that without using this amount, it is impossible to attain the soft, marshmallow-like fluffiness of these dumplings. In addition, most shops add sugar to the roasted soybean flour which traditionally coats this popular dessert. It must be remembered that this kind of sweet extravaganza is partaken of only on special occasions and is certainly not everyday fare. If eaten with this forgiving attitude, you will be surprised at how good it actually tastes.

> 1   cup buckwheat flour (135 g)   **Serves 4**
> 1½   cups water (360 cc) plus ¾ cup sugar (Method A)
>   or
> ¾   cup water (180 cc) and ¾ cup amazake (180 cc)
>   (Method B)
> ½   cup sifted soy flour (65 g)
> ½   cup powdered sugar (65 g)

Choose either of the following methods.

METHOD A: Bring the water to a boil, then add the sugar and stir until it dissolves. Allow it to cool for about 1 minute, or place the whole pan in a larger pan of cold water and stir for about 20 to 30 seconds. Add the buckwheat flour and stir very gently with a wooden spoon 5 or 6 times.

METHOD B: Whip the *amazake* in a blender for 10 seconds, then combine with the buckwheat flour and water.

Heat the mixture over a high flame and mix to make a dough in the same manner as for Soba Dumpling (page 103). If you have achieved the right consistency, you should be able to pull out the dough in one lump.

Moisten your hands in a bowl of cold water, then roughly break the dough into 20 to 24 bite-sized pieces. Rewet your hands as necessary. Roll each ball between your palms until smooth and round. Work as quickly as possible, since the dough will harden within several minutes. Combine the soy flour and sugar. Roll into the soy flour and serve immediately.

Soba Butter Cookies

Butter cookies have been popular in France for centuries. Their popularity stems from their two contrasting textures: a light, crispy crust and a soft, mildly sweet inside.

This variation on the favored French standard calls for buckwheat flour and features buckwheat's grainy quality. To allow the adhesiveness of the buckwheat flour to develop fully, it is important to "put air" into the mixture by tossing it over and over.

2	cups buckwheat flour (270 g)	**Yields 2 dozen**
4	oz butter (1 cube) (115 g)	
6½	Tbsps sugar	
	Pinch salt	
4	tsps vanilla	
6	egg yolks	
⅔	oz cocoa powder (18 g)	

Place the buckwheat flour and softened butter into a bowl and mix together, tossing well.

Let the "grains" fall through your fingertips as you rub your hands together in a light and quick manner. Continue mixing until the overall texture becomes damp and powder-like.

Mix the sugar and salt in another bowl. Add the egg yolks and vanilla, then beat rapidly with an eggbeater in a circular motion until the mixture becomes white and creamy.

Combine the egg mixture with the flour and butter. Mix lightly. After the whole is well blended, form the flour into a dough.

Remove the dough to a cutting board and knead into a ball. Divide into two portions. Add the cocoa to one portion and mix until dough turns a deep brown.

Roll both portions of dough into cylinders 1½ inches in diameter. Wrap tightly in plastic wrap and refrigerate for at least an hour.

Retrieve the cylinders from the refrigerator. Cut them into ⅛-inch-thick slices and place on a greased baking pan. Bake in a preheated oven (340°F) for 7 to 10 minutes or until the edges brown.

Soba Crunch

When buckwheat flour is deep-fried it becomes crispy and makes an ideal snack food. The finished sticks may be coated with syrup, as suggested below, or with honey.

Yields 4 dozen

1½ cups buckwheat flour (200 g)
1⅔ tsps baking powder
4 eggs, lightly beaten
  Vegetable oil for deep-frying
3½ oz brown or black sugar (100 g)
¼ cup water (60 cc)

Mix the flour and baking powder together in a bowl. Make a well in the center of the flour and add the eggs. Knead the mixture until it becomes smooth and satiny. Form into a ball and allow it to rise for at least 1½ hours. Knead well once more.

Roll out dough into ropes about ¼ inch in diameter, then cut into 5-inch lengths.

Preheat the oil and deep-fry the sticks lightly.

To make the syrup, combine the sugar with ¼ cup water in a saucepan over medium heat and stir well until the liquid thickens. Coat deep-fried sticks well. Serve with finger bowl or damp cloth.

Soba Mochi Squares

Hatto

This is another specialty from the village of Hinoemata. Buckwheat flour combined with sweet rice gruel is boiled and then topped with a blend of roasted sesame, cinnamon, and sugar. Served steaming hot, these soft-textured squares make an excellent afternoon snack.

Makes 16–18 squares

2 cups buckwheat flour (270 g)
1 cup sweet rice (mochi-gome) (135 g)
¼ cup sesame seeds (33 g)

2	Tbsps sugar
1	tsp salt
2	tsps cinnamon

Wash the sweet rice, cover in water, and leave to soak for 6 to 8 hours or overnight. Drain well and put in a pan together with 3 cups water. Bring to a boil, cover loosely, and simmer for 45 minutes.

Combine the sesame seeds, sugar, salt, and cinnamon and grind in a mortar and pestle.

Knead the thin sweet-rice gruel into the buckwheat flour. When all of the liquid is absorbed, add $\frac{1}{2}$ to 1 cup water (120 to 240 cc) and then knead until you have soft, sponge-like dough.

Roll out into a rectangle shape about $\frac{1}{4}$ inch thick and cut into 2-inch squares. (If placed in plastic wrap and refrigerated at this point, the uncooked dough will keep for a week.)

Bring ample water to a rapid boil. Place the squares in the boiling water. When they float to the surface, scoop them out.

Coat the boiled squares well with the crushed sesame mix. Serve immediately and eat while they are still hot.

Saké-seasoned Soba Patties

$4\frac{1}{2}$	cups buckwheat flour (600 g)	**Serves 4**
$2\frac{1}{3}$	cups saké (560 cc)	

Bring half of the saké to a boil, then combine over heat with half of the flour as for Soba Dumpling (page 103). Repeat with remaining flour and saké. Form into patties and fry lightly in oil until golden brown on both sides. Serve immediately.

Ingredients

Japanese food continues to gain popularity as an ethnic cuisine. It seems that the more widely it is experienced and understood, the greater is its appeal. The Japanese words *assari* and *sappari*, often used to describe feelings about food, give us a clue as to why this cuisine is finding such broad acceptance. *Assari* refers to a taste that is light and subtle, while *sappari* means that food is amply satisfying and refreshing.

The significance of these words goes a step further. In relation to cooking, they imply that a balance must be struck between rich and light ingredients. *Sappari* encourages us to think of the word "delicious" as entailing not only the initial burst of flavor but also the aftertaste or the way we feel hours after we have left the table.

The ingredients used in soba cuisine offer a whole range of these *assari* and *sappari* foods to enjoy. With time you will be able to use these ingredients, perhaps insignificant when served individually, in combinations that will open up subtle new variations of taste and texture.

Bonito flakes (*katsuo-bushi*): An essential ingredient of the soba master's stock, bonito flakes are shaven from rock-hard pieces of dried bonito, which are either dried and fermented over a 4-month period, or dried, rewashed, and then baked for about 7 to 8 minutes at high temperatures and immediately put through a shredder.

Nowadays, with increasing demand for natural and whole foods, blocks of bonito are becoming more and more readily available in the West. The very best bonito stock is still made from freshly shaved flakes, which requires a special hand slicer. These flakes have an exquisite taste which makes them good garnishes for almost any of the noodle dishes.

When buying flakes, look for those that are neatly shaved, are light in color, and have a nice bacon-like aroma. Once opened, they will keep for about 3 weeks if packed in cellophane and stored in the refrigerator.

Burdock (*gobo*): These roots are harvested from May to February. Good-quality roots are firm and straight, with unblemished skin. The best are without the hole in the center that forms when roots get thick. The skin is the best part of the root, so do not scrape it off but rather scrub with a stiff brush to clean it. In addition, in Japan the leaves are dried, ground, and then added to the buckwheat flour during soba-making, giving a unique viscous quality to the noodles.

Burdock turns dark very quickly after being cut. To avoid discoloration, put the cut burdock into water, preferably with a touch of vinegar in it, as soon as possible.

Daikon radish: This long white stout Japanese radish abounds in vitamin C as well as digestive enzymes, so is cherished for its ability to aid in digestion, especially of foods cooked in oil, like tempura. When cooked and seasoned with the soba broth, the sweetness of this radish comes through. But its main use is as a garnish for the chilled noodles. When grated, it tastes wonderfully hot and refreshing. Connoisseurs prefer it as hot as possible.

When used as a garnish, a radish which is not too watery and has a hot, spicy taste is preferable.

Whereas *wasabi* horseradish is ground from the head to the tip, daikon radish is ground from its tip (which is its hottest point) to the top. As you proceed upward, the daikon becomes more watery and the taste less spicy.

Once it has been grated, the freshness of this root evaporates quickly. It is essential, therefore, to keep it refrigerated in an airtight container once grated. Although only the most conscientious of restaurants will take the trouble to do so, when serving daikon at home try to grate it just before serving.

Daikon sprouts: Large sprouts, used in salads and as a topping on oily dishes.

Fish cakes (*kamaboko*): *Kamaboko* are often used as an appetizer, and as such are a standard part of the *nuki* repertoire at high-class soba establishments (see The Soba Dining Experience). Served with a small dish of soy sauce and freshly grated *wasabi* horseradish, they are the Oriental version of gefilte fish.

Because the cakes can be sliced like salami and eaten "right from the stick," they are used to represent the cheeks in "Rosy-Cheeked" Soba (page 69). Alternatively, they can be simmered in water and eaten as a light snack with cheese and crackers, spread with yellow mustard, or cooked longer and allowed to become soft, as in an *oden* stew.

Flour: Choose your flour carefully. Look for the freshest possible flour and choose the product with the least amount of dark brown specks of ground hull, which gives the flour its slightly bitter taste. Ideally you want flour that has been hulled before the grinding. Japanese millers do this, as do some European makers, and as a result produce a better flour.

Japanese flour is available in as many as seven different grades, ranging from the pure white *sarashina* flour, treasured for its high percentage of pure starch, through the yellowish-green of the middle grades, to the dark chocolate brown of the protein-rich aleuron layer. (see Part I). Since, even under optimum conditions, only 25 percent of the total yield is *sarashina* flour, it is the most costly. (Used as a base in the Flavored Soba Noodles, it is indeed a delicacy with a price). The yellowish-green flour (*seiro*) accounts for roughly 35 percent of the yield, and sells for somewhat less. The chocolate-brown flour (*inakako*) constitutes about 35 percent. The remaining three basic flour types can be combined along with wheat flour in any number of ways to produce an endless variety of soba noodles.

Konbu kelp: Used for its somewhat gelatinizing effect, *konbu* has flat, broad, thick leaves. Brownish-black kelp liberally covered with a fine white powder is a sign of quality. Lightly wipe the surface of kelp with a damp cloth before using it. Store it in an airtight container.

There are a number of processed *konbu* varieties, such as *tororo-konbu*, which also work very well as a quick and tasty supplement for any soba dish requiring a hot broth. Ready-made *konbu*-stock products, often referred to as *konbu dashi*, are also available.

Mirin: *Mirin* is made by extracting the liquid from steamed and fermented sweet rice. Use this smooth-textured sweetener to add depth, taste, and fragrance to any dish.

After fermentation, *mirin* acquires a slight percentage of alcohol. This alcohol content is said to react with the protein in fish and meat, ensuring that it will not break apart so easily while also shortening cooking time by bringing out the flavor more quickly.

Furthermore, when *mirin* is combined with soy sauce or miso and put over a flame, the sweetness of the *mirin* and the amino acids within the soy sauce react to the heat, improving the flavor, glossiness, and color of the mixture.

Before combining it with other ingredients, *mirin* can be placed over a flame by itself and removed just before it reaches the boiling point. This procedure allows the slight alcohol content to evaporate and activates the sweetener and amino acids in the *mirin*, deepening its fragrance while further mellowing its flavor.

Once bottled, the glucose and amino acids in the *mirin* will undergo a chemical reaction if exposed to direct sunlight, and its color will change to a dark brown. Accordingly, store in a cool, dark place.

Miso: Before the turn of the century, soy sauce was at times a luxury item which, in many farming villages like Hinoemata (see "Silk Cut" Soba, page 93), was not available. Throughout these times, miso played a pivotal role in hearty winter dishes such as Soba Noodles in a Miso Stew. With virtually every local area producing its own miso paste since antiquity, the extent of miso's importance can be judged by the sentimental expression *temai-miso*. More than a homage to the miso of one's own area, it carries emotional weight similar to the English expression, "There's no place like home."

Miso comes in three basic types: sweet, medium salty, and salty. In general, white miso is sweet; dark miso is salty. Color ranges along a spectrum from something near ivory to a dark amber, and the salt content varies from about 3 to 15 percent.

Various kinds of miso are now being exported to or made in the United States. American miso companies have sprung up at a grass-roots level and supply multiple flavors and varieties. Professionals as well as homemakers often create blends, easily done by grinding a combination of different pastes in a mortar for a minute or two and experimenting until the desired color and taste are achieved. Once the miso has been opened, store it in an airtight container and refrigerate. White miso keeps approximately 3 months; dark, longer.

Mountain yam (*yama imo*): A variety of potato, shaped like a dog's paw. It has a sweet taste and can be grated to a glutinous consistency.

It is the glutinous texture which makes it the ideal binding agent in Groat and Mountain Yam Fry (page 102). Like daikon, it is considered to be an excellent digestive. Mountain yam is now available at many Japanese food outlets in the West. The standard sweet yam is not a substitute.

***Natto*:** This rich soybean product with a cheese-like flavor is still underestimated, unappreciated, and misunderstood, mainly because the sticky "threads" resulting from its special fermentation process are strong and stubborn, making it pretty tricky for beginners to eat. *Natto* can be made easily at home with soybeans, "*natto* spore" (now available at many major health-food dealers), a pot, and a box. Place the cooked beans in a box, sprinkle with the spore, and let sit overnight. The cooked and "seeded" beans will turn into a fresh batch of the slightly caramel-tasting *natto*. If allowed to sit too long on store shelves, the beans become overripe. Although you cannot check the quality until you open up the package at home, the best *natto* should have a light tannish color and still be moist and a little puffy. Too dark a color indicates overripening and a correspondingly bitter taste. To remedy this situation somewhat, stir the beans together with chopsticks or a spoon and combine with chopped onions, *wasabi* horseradish, and soy sauce. Since this food is the result of bacterial action, no preservative can be used, so *natto* should be eaten as soon as possible.

Nori seaweed: Everyone who has eaten sushi is familiar with these crisp, paper-thin sheets of dried seaweed. *Nori* is as indispensable to the soba-maker as it is to the sushi-maker. Its importance in making Soba Sushi, for example, is easily understood, but its aromatic fragrance, bright sheen, and blackish-purple color (with a hint of green) add a special touch to most soba dishes. It is used in virtually all the cold and many of the hot noodle recipes in this book. *Nori* is best stored in a tightly sealed can to keep out moisture and sunlight. Precut strips of toasted or flavored *nori* are also on the market, but it is better to use standard-size sheets, toasting and cutting them yourself just before using to capture their distinctive fragrance.

To toast a sheet of *nori*, pass it back and forth over a medium flame several times. Within 10 to 15 seconds, the surface will become shiny and the *nori* will emit a nice fragrance. Turn off the heat and tear the sheet into bite-size pieces.

Okara: One of Japan's most neglected foods (even in Japan), *okara* is the ground soybean pulp that remains after the curd has been drained away. It should be used the same day it is made, and so is best obtained from a local tofu maker or distributor.

Okara combines well with other foods with strong flavors, as it has very little flavor of its own. Keep wrapped and refrigerated until ready to use.

Potato starch (*katakuriko*): This is a starch made from the sweet or white potato. It is used to make thick, clear sauces, but should be used only in dishes that are going to be eaten the same day, as it "leaks" water. Since potato starch is stronger than cornstarch, substitute $1\frac{1}{2}$ Tbsps cornstarch for 1 Tbsp potato starch.

Salmon roe (*ikura*): Used in Western as well as Eastern countries for its taste and bright orange color, salmon roe was once discarded in the United States. Now, of course, it has found favor as a sushi topping. Similarly, it makes an ideal topping for Soba Sushi or for a simple bowl of noodles in broth.

Sesame seeds: There are various uses for sesame seeds in soba cookery. As a garnish, they lend a nutty fragrance and are thus used to help bring out the sweetness of, say, the *natto* in the Cold Soba Noodles with Natto and Sesame recipe. Another use is to grind the seeds into paste and mix them into the chilled dipping sauce with a touch of freshly grated ginger, creating a refreshing sauce sure to ease the dog days of summer.

There are both white and black sesame seeds. Black sesame has a slightly stronger flavor, while the white is slightly more oily. When using sesame as a garnish, choose the color that looks best—black on green vegetables, white or black on rice, and so on.

Try to obtain the whole seed, as once it is cracked open it can easily go rancid. Keep seeds in an airtight container free from moisture.

Seven-flavor spice (*shichimi togarashi*): This aromatic mixture of spices is composed of red pepper flakes, dried mandarin peel, white poppy seed, powdered *sansho*, hemp seed, and *shiso* or green *nori* seaweed. It is great on any of the hot noodle dishes and is a standard condiment at any soba shop.

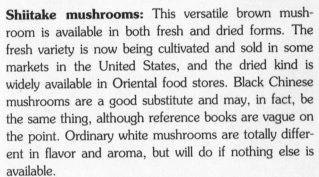

Shiitake mushrooms: This versatile brown mushroom is available in both fresh and dried forms. The fresh variety is now being cultivated and sold in some markets in the United States, and the dried kind is widely available in Oriental food stores. Black Chinese mushrooms are a good substitute and may, in fact, be the same thing, although reference books are vague on the point. Ordinary white mushrooms are totally different in flavor and aroma, but will do if nothing else is available.

When buying fresh shiitake, look for caps that are curled under, not opened out. The undersides of the caps should be whitish. Brown or mottled undersides indicate old mushrooms. The thicker the mushroom, the better. Some get so thick that the tops of the caps split and crack, and these are the best quality. There are spring and fall crops, but the spring mushrooms are better, with thicker flesh and a stronger aroma.

Dried mushrooms are sold whole, cut into strips, or in crumbled or powdered form. Thick flesh and good aroma (you can usually sniff and tell if the aroma is good even if packaged in clear plastic) are the criteria for good dried shiitake. Reconstitute in tepid water until soft.

Reconstitution time will vary greatly with the thickness and size of the mushrooms, but calculate 2 to 3 hours for good mushrooms. A shorter soaking time is possible if the shiitake are to be used in simmered foods.

Unlike white mushrooms, the stems of shiitake are tough and must be removed from both fresh and dried mushrooms. Reserve these for soup stock if you wish.

Shiso: Although two varieties of *shiso* exist, soba professionals most often use the green variety. It accompanies many of the appetizers served at the high-class soba restaurants and is used in making Flavored Soba Noodles. Its minty and aromatic fragrance seems to fit soba like a glove.

Soy Sauce: Soy sauce is made from soybeans, wheat, and a saltwater mixture. It is the major ingredient in the broth that accompanies soba noodles in Japan. Like miso and saké, several varieties have been developed over the centuries. In addition to the so-called regular, dark-colored soy sauce, lighter, milder (low-sodium for those who must restrict their intake of salt), and even sweet varieties have joined the ranks of standard products on store shelves.

Soy sauce contains a high percentage of amino acids, notably glutamine acid (also present in *konbu*), which provides its distinctive and pleasing taste.

The recipes in this book call for regular or, on

occasion, light-colored soy sauce. These sauces are brewed in the traditional way, which entails a 6-to-12-month fermentation period. The process can be speeded up by adding alcohol (for example), thereby shortening the fermentation to a period of three months or less. In addition, these recipes have been conceived with naturally brewed Japanese soy sauce in mind. Chinese soy sauce will not work. Beware also of synthetic soy sauces, often with Chinese-sounding names, that use additional ingredients to hasten the fermentation process. Needless to say, these are not the varieties that will yield a soba broth worth raving about here.

Actually, I had the chance to prepare homemade soy sauce while living with Mr. Noboru Muramoto (author of *Healing Ourselves*) from 1971 to 1975. As in cultivating a garden, you must attend to the sauce faithfully, stirring it twice a day (morning and night) to ensure the proper blending of the ingredients. After about 3 months Muramoto-san's whole garage started to exude the sweetest caramel-like fragrance. Scooping out some of the "living" soy-wheat mixture and using it in bread-making not only makes it into a meal in itself but also works as a "natural" rising agent in place of yeast. Although you may balk at making your own soy sauce, the results are worth the effort. Grassroots production of soy sauce is still in its infancy in America, but it's possible to buy a wide variety of quality soy sauce products made by Kikkoman.

Thin deep-fried tofu: see tofu, thin deep-fried.

Tofu: The history of soybean cuisine in America began with grass-roots efforts in the 1970s. The ever-adaptable soybean stands proud as a giant industry in the United States today. Having sprung up in towns across the nation, tofu-makers continue to break new ground with such adaptations as the New York–born tofutti (ice cream made from soybeans and natural flavorings). With ingenuity like this, other nutritious and scrumptious uses of the soybean will undoubtedly emerge.

The sizes of tofu cakes in the United States apparently vary. Of the various types of tofu used in soba cuisine, deep-fried tofu of different kinds (see below) is used most often. The Soy-Soba Noodle recipe calls for soaked and mashed raw soybeans, but in the northern Iwate prefecture, a block of regular or "cotton" tofu is added directly into the buckwheat flour with 2 or 3 egg yolks and, with only a little water, is mixed together into a dough. Store tofu blocks in clean water and use within 2 days, changing the water often.

Tofu, thin deep-fried (*aburi-age, usu-age*): This ingredient appears frequently in soba cooking, but the most famous use is in the dish "Fox" (*Kitsune*) Soba. In Japan, as in the West, foxes are thought to be keen and cunning and somewhat daring. These characteristics were also necessary for temple cooks, who constantly had to create ways of preparing food that would satisfy like meat without containing any. Since this fried variety of tofu is rich in oil, when cooked together with the flavoring sauce it takes on a sweet, bacon-like taste, satisfying the diner who won't sense anything missing. (See

"Fox" Soba, page 73, for preparation.) Thin, deep-fried tofu should be sealed in plastic wrap and refrigerated. It will keep 1 week in this manner. Larger amounts will keep 2 to 3 months if frozen.

Wakame seaweed: This green, ribbon-like sea vegetable's slippery-smooth texture and delightful fragrance make it extremely popular, and in fact Wakame Soba is served at a great majority of the stand-up soba shops throughout Japan. Soak as you would *konbu* and allow to cook in the broth for 2 to 3 minutes. It also combines well with salads or appetizers, and in this book is called for in the Groat Salad with Vinegar Dressing (page 99).

A superb health food rich in calcium, fresh *wakame* appears on the market only in the spring, but dried *wakame* is available year-round. There are a number of varieties, but in every case the best *wakame* should have a dark, blackish-green color. Store in cellophane in a cool, dark place.

Wasabi horseradish: By no means the exclusive domain of the sushi maker, this variety of horseradish is indispensable to soba cuisine as well. Releasing a sharp, tangy taste when grated into paste, *wasabi* is a standard condiment for cool dishes. Together with white radish and long onions, it forms the trio of garnishes that are considered so essential to soba cuisine that they are simply referred to as "the three tastes" (*san-shoku*) by shops in Tokyo.

There are two kinds of *wasabi*: that produced in clear-mountain-water areas and that which grows in fields. The former is the variety that is by and large in supply and demand.

The *wasabi* root is green in color, strong in fragrance, and, when ground, hot and spicy. Compared with field *wasabi*, that produced in clear mountain water has obviously superior characteristics. While the former has a dry, harsh taste, the latter acquires a fine balance between its pungent and sweet qualities.

To grate the *wasabi* root, first cut off the top leaves and sharpen the head like shaving a pencil. Scrape the hard impacted dirt and skin off the portion to be grated using the dull side of a knife. With a sturdy metal grater, grind from top to bottom.

Once *wasabi* is grated, it keeps for only a short time. Since about 15 to 20 portions can be obtained from one root, you probably won't use a whole one at a time, except for a party. So, after grating the portion needed, store the rest. By placing it in a bin of cool water, you can keep it from losing its fragrance for at least 24 hours.

Because the fresh root is so expensive, powdered *wasabi* has become an acceptable alternative. Powdered *wasabi* is made from a different type of horseradish and includes cayenne pepper (*togarashi* in Japanese). Consequently, it is sharper and less subtle than fresh *wasabi*. To use, add enough water to make a thick paste, then cover for 10 minutes to allow the flavor to mature.

Yuzu citron: This unique variety of citron originated in China. Belonging to the orange family, its tall evergreen tree produces a yellow fruit in winter and a green one if harvested in early autumn. Only its outer skin is used, as the fruit itself is too bitter. The skin, on the other hand, imparts a fruity "sweet-lemon" flavor.

Put into chilled broth, *yuzu* enhances the light and refreshing feeling of the broth. When put into hot broth, it creates a delicately aromatic fragrance. In addition, it is said to be effective in lightening the oily feeling of dishes containing fish or animal products, and is almost always used in soba dishes with tempura, chicken, or duck.

Generally the zest is peeled off in a round, semicircular motion, piece by piece. The size of the piece, left up to each master to decide, can be as big as a nickel or as small as a sunflower seed. When used to accompany side dishes, it is often peeled extra large, thinly sliced, and piled on top of crisp tempura or lightly fried and seasoned chicken. A very simple, refreshing side dish, traditionally served in Japanese cooking, is made simply by combining finely sliced *yuzu* skin together with grated daikon radish. When *nameko* mushrooms (small, tasty mushrooms floating in their own syrup) are added, this becomes *nameko-oroshi*, also a standard side dish of great popularity. In like manner, *yuzu* can be added as that "something extra" to give Western salads a little more life.

One of its most unusual uses, however, is to puree the skin (without pulp) in a food processor and then knead it together with the highly refined, pure-white *sarashina* buckwheat flour. This combination produces a popular variety among the style of buckwheat noodles known as *kawari soba* (see Flavored Soba Noodles, page 80). It provides a noodle with a refreshing hint of citrus taste and a beautiful bright-yellow color. (Only the yellow winter variety is used for this style of noodles.) Once again, taking a hint from this method, try adding blended *yuzu* into breads, cookies, cakes, or pastries.

Serving Ware and Tools

*T*he various serving utensils of the soba shop have their specific functional uses while also contributing to the overall ambience of the eating experience. The essential tools of the trade are the large lacquered bowl, the light-weight rolling pin, and the hefty straight-edged knife to allow for the experienced soba maker to produce picture-perfect noodles.

Trays (seiro, zaru)

Bowls (*donburi*)

Dipping cups (*choko*)

Sauce bottles (*tokkuri*)

Pitchers for *soba-yu* (*yuto*)

Condiment containers

Tools

Mixing bowl

Knife

Rolling pins

II

SOBA
DINING

The Soba Dining Experience

Soba is mainly thought of as a food to eat on the run. It is an ideal light lunch or snack because it can be prepared at short notice and is nourishing as well as easily digested. Yet, the better soba shops also attract an evening clientele, and these more discriminating customers are not in such a hurry. On the contrary, they come in search of a quiet place in which to enjoy solitude or companionship, a flask of saké, and good, honest fare at leisure.

"Saki ni, sake dake dashite morau!"

("Anyway, to start with, just bring the saké!")

Traditional soba shops provide light fare, which makes a perfect accompaniment (as it turns out) for saké. Granting, of course, that menus vary slightly from shop to shop, one of the standard ways to start is simply to order a glass of cold or hot saké (depending on the season). In the next breath, order a plate of sliced Rolled Omelette (*Tamago-yaki* in Japanese). At first glance, the omelette closely resembles those made at sushi shops. But just one bite is enough to experience the superior broth of the soba master. Not just sweet, this omelette is much juicier and richer. Some restaurants whip up a fresh batch on order, in which case three to five minutes are necessary to receive a steaming serving of thick, juicy slices.

While eating the omelette slices, the saké begins to entice the senses. As the desire to order another flask arises, order the dish called *nuki* along with it. *Nuki* literally means "left out," not indicating at first just what ingredient is omitted. At traditional soba shops, there are two standard types of *nuki*, chicken or duck *nuki* and tempura *nuki*. *Tori-nuki* (chicken) or *kamo-nuki* (duck) refer to bowls of soup which contain fresh and supple pieces of chicken or duck sautéed with sliced Welsh onions. No soba noodles. No soba anything. Then there is *ten-nuki*. This refers to a bowl of soup with only tempura-fried shrimp. Here, too, the soba is missing. The *nuki* serves as a light soup, imparting a hint of flavor to whet the appetite and complement the saké.

Whatever appetizer is served, it is important that it have a clear and decisive taste. The *nuki* broth, which uses regular soy sauce, assuredly falls into this category. As the warmth of the saké begins to relax you, take one swig of the soup, and all trace or memory of saké disappears. But then the soup begins to tease, creating a pleasant, almost haunting thirst that only saké can quench (or so it seems). In other words, it is doing its job as an appetizer, encouraging one to eat, yet leaving room for another few drinks. If you make it to one of the shops in this book, where the cooks are top-notch, you will also greatly appreciate the high-quality oil used for the duck, chicken, or tempura.

Nuki pleases in the same manner as a crafted English sports car. From the outside the car looks stylish and fancy, but on the other hand, it's at first awkward to drive. In the beginning the gears don't mesh, or the clutch doesn't engage, for example, and you are wondering whether this car is worth all the rave it has been accorded. Yet, as you begin to master its idiosyncrasies and become confident enough to take it for a cruise on the highway, you feel for the first time the pleasure and magnificence of the machine that you are driving. The car hugs the road nicely, and the engine sounds great as it is being wound out.

Order another flask of saké.

By the time you have finished the substantial part of the *nuki* dish (that is, the chewy duck or chicken or the crispy fried shrimp), the light consommé-like broth has "absorbed" some of the tempura batter or natural oils of the fowl. Before you know it, a thick and strong-tasting stew has formed.

Now is the time to add the hot and sweet-tasting cooking water of soba, called *soba-yu* in Japanese, to the remaining broth. *Soba-yu* is not only added for the purpose of diluting the thickened soup: it provides the fragrance of soba. Drop by drop, this soup is very strong and thick. But it is made with precision, embodying the spirit of the shop. This taste is said to be the real taste of Tokyo.

I'll never forget the first meeting I had with Dr. Tsuji, (introduced later in the Nutrition section). "The mark of good *nuki* is that it retains its sharp taste down to the last drop of this *soba-yu* soup," he told me. "Never forget to drink *soba-yu* whenever you eat soba. It contains an abundance of buckwheat's water-soluble proteins and B vitamins."

You can't disguise the taste of a *nuki* soup. By adding *soba-yu*, the diluted broth and the quality of the bonito and soy sauce become even more obvious. Shops which take pride in their *nuki* generally make soup that alone is worth the price of the meal.

Needless to say, soba restaurants that offer good *nuki* present a broth (and dipping sauce) of high quality. In Japan, the soup of such and such an area or place is always a popular topic of discussion among soba-lovers. "What is the ratio of ingredients in his soup?"—this question is an indication that the soba maker is widely acknowledged for more than just the noodles themselves.

The technique of making delicious *nuki* is still alive and indeed experiencing a comeback in popularity. Yet, keep in mind that most of the regular soba shops are more fast-food–oriented and do not offer *nuki*. As it requires technique, experience, and sense, the art of making good *nuki* places the professional soba shop in an entirely different category.

As George Ohsawa said, "Everything that has a beginning has an end." In many of the more ordinary soba shops today, if you walk in and ask for *nuki*, they will be at a loss to understand you. It would be forgivable if they would just admit that they don't know the meaning of *nuki*. But to reply that "We don't serve that kind of food here" or, after a long discussion among the chefs as to what the customer wants, to bring out plain, hot *kake soba*, thinking that *ten-nuki* means noodles without tempura! *Nuki* is much different from poor-man's soba.

Whenever you are out in the Tokyo area in the early evening hours, whether in a group or alone, visit the shops selected in this book and enjoy the customary *nuki* with saké before or during your order of soba. It will provide a most extraordinary taste experience and add to your appreciation of soba and saké at the same time.

Selected Soba Restaurants in Japan

As a well-traveled photographer friend of mine once quipped, "My favorite restaurants are those which serve large portions at low prices." Certainly, many factors come into play when deciding what and where to eat. Other than price, some obvious considerations are convenience, environment, and the quality of service of the restaurant. Last, but certainly not least, come the taste and nutritional content of the food. While many restaurant reviews classify and award stars or points to differentiate one shop from another, it cannot be denied that personal preferences will lead to two entirely different reactions to the same place.

Sometimes when you are running around a big city like Tokyo (or New York or Chicago) you want a light but satisfying meal. In Japan, men and women, businessmen and students, young and old alike satisfy this need by dropping into the nearest soba stand, usually located near or within any train station. There they can get a big bowl of steaming hot noodles with loads of *wakame*, vegetables, or tempura toppings for about the price of a sandwich.

Soba stands constitute about 45 percent of the 41,000 soba shops in Japan today; "town shops," featuring machine-made noodles, make up an additional

45 percent; and the special traditional soba shops that serve handmade noodles account for about 10 percent. While the ingredients used in soba cuisine at any level are basically decided through tradition, differences in the quality and ratios of these ingredients, as well as individual cooking styles and techniques of masters, enable each stand, restaurant, or unique "hideaway" to maintain its own unique taste. By taking a look at the two fundamental elements within soba cuisine—the noodle itself and the broth which accompanies it—we can understand precisely the differences which provide the "special" taste featured at each restaurant.

Soba stands (*tachi gui*) serve noodles that contain only 30 to 40 percent buckwheat and are made at a factory with cheaper flour, yet provide a satisfying quick meal. In all honesty, some of these establishments serve pretty mediocre stuff, but before you dismiss soba as good for nothing but a cheap meal on the run, try another place, one a little more upmarket. In fact, I have often heard newcomers to Japan rave that their local stand serves "such a tasty bowl of noodles, all for $2.00!" when actually it is the taste of the soup which keeps them coming back for more. Soup stocks vary from stand to stand, with some producing quite tasty broths. Keep in mind when entering these places that you can order a variety of toppings to go with your noodles. For example, a *kitsune-wakame-tamago* combination (thin deep-fried tofu, *wakame* seaweed, and egg) can be ordered instead of just one ingredient. On the average, the price of a tray of soba is about ¥250 to ¥300; with tempura, ¥320 to ¥380.

Next in number are soba shops that serve machine-made

soba in town centers and also deliver to your home. I used to rely heavily on these establishments for my daily meals, either dropping by or calling for home delivery. By and large family-managed affairs, each one has its own homey taste and appeal. A great majority display models of plastic soba outside the restaurant, rendering them easily identifiable. The quality is usually considerably better than that of the soba stands, and the price is accordingly about two to three times higher. They feature soba that has been made either at the factory or on the premises by the master. The noodles contain 50 to 70 percent buckwheat (and 30 to 50 percent wheat), and are much more elastic than the "stand" variety. Their long and thin, easily digestible texture provides a satisfyingly light meal. I was grateful for the soba home-delivery service during those many times when cooking was out of the question. These soba shops employ various methods for the soup stock, using medium- to high-grade ingredients and often using the bonito twice after allowing it to dry. The price of a tray of plain soba is about ¥430 to ¥480; and with tempura, ¥750 to ¥850.

Finally, we come to the traditional handmade-soba restaurants. It is from this group that we have selected the restaurants reviewed here. Traditional soba restaurants constitute less than 10 percent of the whole, or roughly 4,000 restaurants, which is why so few people have ever enjoyed the experience of eating fine soba. At the most traditional of these establishments, the soba noodles are made completely by hand using only a mixing bowl, rolling pin, board, and knife. Others, which deal in a large volume, use a mixing machine in the beginning, and sometimes even a cutting aid at the end.

Some shops place greater emphasis on the quality of the other ingredients. Of the establishments serving exclusively handmade soba, only about 10 percent follow the adage "First year, mixing; second year, rolling; third year, cutting." Those that do are usually headed by a soba master. On this count, there are perhaps 400 soba masters in Japan today, many of whom have become quite famous, attracting not only a wide clientele but also apprentices, one of whom will be allowed to carry on each shop's name.

However, the differentiation does not end there. We can even say that of these 400 masters, only 10 to 15 percent offer soba flour ground fresh that day. *If you experience soba made from this flour, you will have eaten soba noodles at their absolute best!* (Many shops claim to make handmade, or *te-uchi*, noodles, but, as explained in the History section, the term has become so abused and overused that it is expected by the customer who frequents any nicely decorated soba shop, whether the noodles are handmade or not.)

Few in number, but sharp and biting as the *wasabi* they grate, these masters carry on the traditions of Japanese soba cooking in the spirit of sumo—that is, by a strictly controlled and retained ranking system which, while unspoken, pervades the circles attached to the soba master. There are "*yokozuna*" (established masters of 20 or more years with considerable fame and following), "*ozeki*" (10 to 15 years, opening their own shops after years of training), "*sekiwake*" (3 to 10 years of training), and "*maegashira*" (trainees). Each of them takes pride in delivering soba according to his own understanding and preferences. Again, as with sumo, many of the masters are born into the "way," and other "newcomers" struggle to get to the top, branching off to spread their master's style of soba-making in their own direction.

While one can learn the stand and machine styles of soba preparation in just a short period of time, the handmade style takes years of training to acquire. What qualifications distinguish good soba shops from the also-rans? Traditionalists and modern soba chefs alike agree that to produce the best soba, the principles encapsulated in the phrase "*Hiki-tate, uchi-tate, yude-tate*" must be upheld. According to this adage the ideal soba is obtained by "using freshly ground flour, making the soba within 2 to 3 hours of serving, and serving it within 1 minute of cooking." (An exception is Soy-Soba Noodles in the Country Cooking section.)

Interestingly, nowadays there is a new trend of soba stands proudly displaying signboards claiming to serve soba which satisfies the above three ideal standards. A modern-day version of traditional soba uses soba flour that contains only 30 to 50 percent buckwheat. It is served right upon boiling (*yude-tate*), using machine noodles made fresh that day (*uchi-tate*), from flour ordered from a specialty miller (*hiki-tate*).

They use a lighter-tasting broth, the quality of the accompanying ingredients is high, and they are freshly prepared. As customers line up for this fare day in and day out, one can see that there must be something to this slogan. Less elaborate technique and less refined ingredients notwithstanding, the customers know the taste of good, fresh soba and recognize that for the price these new soba stands are offering a good deal.

Even taking this development into account, however, it's still possible to divide traditional soba-making into two broad categories, *yabu* and *sarashina*, which boast histories of one and two centuries, respectively.

The *yabu* style features soba which has been made from a rough grinding of the whole buckwheat grain; it is dark in color and sweet in taste. This is the style of soba as it first evolved. A popular and economical fare among laborers of old Tokyo, it originally had a low-class image. The soup which accompanies this soba is made from the "regular" dark soy sauce, which is the basic component in the taste of Tokyo (where lie the roots of the soba business) and which was favored as a good complement to the sweet taste of the dark-colored noodles.

The *sarashina* style features soba made from the center of the grain only. As explained in detail in the Characteristics section, only 18 percent of the buckwheat kernel is made up of this high-grade starch. Correspondingly, the price of this flour is three times that of the more abundant dark-colored flour. This *sarashina* flour is pure-white and is either served as a plain white noodle or combined with black sesame seeds, the yellow skin of the *yuzu* citron, and green *shiso* leaves to attain brightly colored Flavored Soba. As the pure-white noodle has an imperceptible taste by itself, the soup which accompanies it is milder than that of the *yabu* style.

Traditional soba shops use only carefully selected ingredients for their stock, paying special attention to making the best taste at a slightly higher cost. In addition, the elegance of the restaurants (interior, utensils, tables, and so on) is also top-class. They use homemade flour (ground fresh daily) or flour of the highest grade (see Characteristics). The noodles contain 70 to 90 percent buckwheat (30 to 10 percent wheat). The price of a tray of plain soba is about ¥800 to ¥1,200; and with tempura, ¥1,000 to ¥2,400, depending on the amount and quality of the tempura ingredients.

To differentiate further these elite 40 to 50 shops would take us beyond the scope of this introductory book on soba. Personal preference, background, and experience will lead you to discover your own favorites. In addition, as apprentices gain confidence and skill, little shops spring up each year like bamboo shoots, making it almost impossible to mention all of the shops worthy of their trade.

Therefore, while not being the last word on the subject, the reviews in this book represent soba that upholds the three *tates* mentioned above, and will not fail to deliver entrées which will confirm all the claims made for soba in this book.

NOTE: The usage of soba terms for Soba Noodles in a Basket (Mori Soba, or *Seiro*, or *Zaru*), as well as other names, varies slightly from shop to shop. To facilitate your ordering at the soba restaurants included here, the shop's preferred phrasing has been used.

Honjinbo

Amano Bldg., B1, 1-5-10 Nishi-Shinbashi, Minato-ku, Tokyo
☎ (03) 3508–8166

NEAREST STATION: Uchisaiwaicho Station, Mita Line; Shinbashi
Station, various lines

HOURS: 11:00–21:30; Saturdays and holidays, 11:00–20:00;
closed Sundays

After eight successful years in Shinbashi, Honjinbo moved to
its present location in Nishi-Shinbashi. The menu features
buckwheat noodles rolled out and cut by hand in the traditional
way. If you have always thought that all soba noodles are the
same, this shop's menu will be an eye-opener.

Honjinbo's trademark is the daily production of three styles
of soba: "plain" (*seiro*), colored (*sarashina*), and thick, dark-
brown country-style noodles (*inaka soba*). Honjinbo uses only
top-quality buckwheat flours. The plain *seiro* soba, which is
light in color, is cut very thin and made from a 2-to-8 ratio of
wheat to buckwheat. Thinly cut, colored soba combines the
pure white inner flour of the buckwheat with fragrant condiments such as yellow *yuzu* citron, green *shiso* leaves, or black
sesame seeds. The chewy, "country-style" soba features the
outer chocolate-brown, protein-rich, sweet flour.

Offered in either regular or large (*omori*) sizes, the soba
can be ordered individually, two kinds served back to back, or
three kinds served one by one. Just as you are finishing your
first tray, the second will appear. The third comes just as you
are finishing your second, with uncanny timing.

The pleasure of this method of delivery is that although all
the noodles have been made from buckwheat, they each look
good and have a distinctive taste and texture, meaning that
you never tire of the always fresh and spicy servings. The
accompanying broth is not as strong as the *yabu* style, but
nevertheless stimulating and delicious. In addition, the soup stock
for the cool noodles is kept at just the right temperature for
the time of year. In summer, you'll never fail to get a refresh-
ingly chilled soup stock. This may sound like a small point, but
if you've ever received a lukewarm soup on a hot Tokyo summer day, you'll appreciate the difference. The same goes for the

Tokyo soba shop, exterior view

temperature of the soba which is dashed over and over again with ice water. The beer and saké are also properly chilled.

Ten Seiro (fresh noodles with a serving of tempura) features two big pieces of crisp and crunchy shrimp, which can be eaten tail and all, accompanied by eggplant and small green pepper. Green tea, which is made individually and served before the meal, is another indication of quality.

With the opening of his new restaurant, Honjinbo's master assembled a staff of expert chefs to handle the appetizer (*nuki*) cooking, and now offers a variety of dishes, some of which change each week, including Soba Miso, Soba Sushi, and Soba Dumpling (takeout service is also available). This is an experience in fine Japanese dining, featuring the best in buckwheat. Don't miss it.

How to get there: Take the A3 exit heading for Toranomon. At the top of the stairs go toward the crosswalk about 50 yards ahead. Honjinbo is located alongside on the left-hand side, in the basement, and a big house-shaped sign makes its location easily identifiable. From Shinbashi Station, it is a 5- to 7-minute walk down Sotobori-dori heading toward the Hibiya Center. Honjinbo will be on the right-hand side.

Honke Owari-ya

Nijo Minami Hairu, Kurumaya-cho, Nakagyo-ku, Kyoto
☎ (075) 231–3446
NEAREST STATION: Oike Station, Karasuma Line
HOURS: 11:00–19:00, closed Wednesdays

This Kyoto soba restaurant is one of the oldest of the old. Established some 527 years ago, it is renowned for maintaining the traditional ways.

The most popular dish is a mini-*Wanko Soba* affair called *Horai Soba* for ¥1,800, which is served with generous amounts of daikon radish (mounded in the center) surrounded by equally generous portions of shrimp tempura, freshly grated *wasabi* horseradish, bonito flakes, *nori*, and sesame seeds.

How to get there: Walk down Karasuma-dori heading toward Nijo-dori. You'll find the shop after 2 to 3 minutes, on your right.

Honmura-an

2–7–11 Kamiogi, Suginami-ku, Tokyo
☎ (03) 3390–0325
NEAREST STATION: Ogikubo Station, JR Chuo Line
HOURS: 11:00–21:00, closed Thursdays

Third-generation master Katsuro began making the homemade style of service twenty-four years ago. He is one of the pioneers in home milling and is a highly respected leader of the soba movement in Japan. Using the best domestic harvest of buckwheat, he stone-grinds only what flour is necessary for that day's business (keeping the groats in a cooled warehouse) and proceeds faithfully to follow the famous motto of "freshly ground, freshly made, freshly cooked." Since he uses a rough grind, the noodles are shorter than at other places. This is another demonstration of educating customers to the merits of a distinctive style. Once again, order large *omori* portions to begin with.

Eating on tatami at Homura-an, Tokyo

How to get there: Go out the exit nearest Nishi-Ogikubo Station, turn left after passing through the wicket, then right on Kanjo Hachi-go road, the lane that parallels the tracks. You'll see a big billboard indicating the location of the shop, with a map. It takes about 10 minutes on foot. If this proves to be too difficult, take a 3-minute taxi ride.

Issa-an

1–8–24 Yuki-no-shita, Kamakura, Kanagawa Prefecture
☎ (0467) 22-3556
NEAREST STATION: Kamakura Station, Yokosuka Line
HOURS: 11:00–19:00, closed some Thursdays

Set around a courtyard with stone lanterns and a fence of bamboo, this shop was a residence in the Taisho period (1912–1926). The atmosphere is suitable for an ancient city like Kamakura, where many tourists come to breathe the air of a Japan from times gone by. Fortunately, this store doesn't take advantage of its attractive location to skimp on making good-quality soba. Instead, they use the best soba flour available from Hokkaido, as well as from Aomori and Ibaraki prefectures. Tea-flavored Soba is ¥1,350, and Kawari Soba is

¥1,000. In summer, *Seiro Soba* (¥820) is recommended; in winter, try the Wild Duck Soba (*Kamo Nanban Soba*). According to season, Yellow Chinese Citron (*Yuzu*) Soba, Black Sesame (*Goma*) Soba, and Green Mugwort (*Yomogi*) Soba are offered and recommended.

How to get there: Walk down Sando street toward the Hachiman-gu temple. After 5 to 6 minutes you'll see two large parking lots on the left. The shop is located next door.

Kuro Mugi

Shin Aoyama Bldg., B1, 1–1–1 Minami Aoyama, Minato-ku, Tokyo
☎ (03) 3475–1850
NEAREST STATION: Aoyama 1-chome Station, Ginza Line
HOURS: 11:30–20:30; Saturdays and holidays until 19:00; holidays, 11:30–19:00; closed Sundays

Kuro mugi means "black wheat" and is one of buckwheat's nicknames. Indeed, this store lives up to its name and serves soba which only a specialist can prepare. Most popular and representative of the dishes served is the entrée *Sanshoku Soba* (green tea, poppy seed, and regular *seiro*, ¥1,200). They have a beautiful mural of old Edo along one of the walls, and the waitresses are sharp and attentive, so if you work in this area, count yourself lucky and step in for some honest-to-goodness handmade soba.

How to get there: Exit Aoyama 1-chome Station and follow the signs to Aoyama Twin Towers.

Masu-oto

2–25–18 Hirai, Edogawa-ku, Tokyo
☎ (03) 3681–5610
NEAREST STATION: Hirai Station, JR Sobu Line
HOURS: 12:00–18:30, closed Thursdays

The master, Hiroyuki Suzuki, has traveled extensively throughout Japan in search of ever-new ways to prepare soba. Over a career spanning sixty years, he has kept detailed notes of his travels and observations about soba. Convinced that the best soba shops never alter their style according to the whims of the customers (who are endlessly saying that the broth should be this way or the noodle that), Suzuki serves modest but graceful portions and in addition has purposely chosen to keep his shop dimly lit and sparsely heated in the winter or too warm in the summer, as if to challenge the customer to enjoy the taste of the soba in as natural a setting as possible. In addition, the colorful artifacts and paintings from the Edo period convincingly evoke the Tokyo of old.

Noodles made from 100-percent buckwheat flour soba are the master's choice. Using flour from Nagano and Ibaraki (two of the most famous buckwheat regions in Japan), Master Suzuki presents noodles a little thicker than *yabu*, with a nice sweet taste. Noodles on a Tray (*Mori Soba*) are ¥600; with tempura, ¥1,800.

How to get there: Walk straight down the Shopping Mall (*shoten-gai*) for 3 to 5 minutes and you'll find the shop on your right.

Matsuya

1–13, Kanda Suda-cho, Chiyoda-ku, Tokyo
☎ (03) 3251–1556
NEAREST STATION: Awajicho Station, Marunouchi Line; Ogawa-machi Station, Shinjuku Line
HOURS: 11:00–20:00, closed Sundays and holidays

Located in the heart of Kanda, this shop has been run by the same family for three generations. They use high-quality soba flour to make the noodles in the traditional way.

The Kodaka family has been traditional soba-makers since 1884. Toshi Kodaka, Matsuya's third-generation proprietor, continues the traditional ways of the shop, whose name means "Pine House" in English. From the monumental bowl for kneading soba dough—carved from horse chestnut wood, dark and glossy with age—to the rustic bamboo and mud-plastered walls, the dark wood ceiling, and the paper-shaded lamps,

Matsuya exudes the air of the old Tokyo soba shop and provides a soothing respite from Kanda's busy streets.

At Matsuya, dark buckwheat flour is kneaded with egg yolks to make a rich, brown noodle. Matsuya relies on a 5-to-1 ratio of buckwheat to wheat flour, with the eggs as an additional binding agent. Matsuya's dipping sauce is a variation on the *yabu* style. The connoisseur could be completely satisfied with the simplest order, Soba Noodles in a Basket— *Hanamaki Soba*. This dish is a stringent test of the quality of soba, since the noodles must stand on their own. Matsuya passes the test, a result of using only the best domestic buckwheat flour and freshly grated *wasabi* horseradish from Izu. *Hanamaki Soba* appears on a small lacquer tray, with a dish of chopped scallions and grated *wasabi*, a pot of dipping sauce, a cup, and chopsticks. Glossy, greenish-black flakes of *nori* seaweed are scattered over the tangle of soba. Other cold soba dishes include *Mori Soba* (without *wasabi* or *nori*), *Taroro Soba* (noodles served with the grated yam and *wasabi*), and *Tenzaru* (noodles and hot tempura).

Matsuya's menu of hot soba dishes runs the gamut from *Kitsune* ("Fox") *Soba* to *Okame* ("Rosy-Cheeked") *Soba*. They also offers a very delicious Soba Dumpling (¥950), which has become quite a rarity at soba shops these days.

How to get there: Take the A3 exit and walk down Yasukuni street for 2 to 3 minutes heading toward Sudacho Street. Matsuya will be on the left-hand side.

Muromachi Sunaba

4–1–13 Muromachi, Nihonbashi, Chuo-ku, Tokyo
☎ (03) 3241–4038
NEAREST STATION: Kanda Station, various lines
HOURS: Weekdays, 11:00–19:30; Saturday, 11:00–19:00; closed
    Sundays, holidays, and third Saturday of each month

The original Sunaba is credited as having been one of the first, if not the first, famous soba shops in Japan. This branch of Sunaba (which signifies another family or style in addition to *yabu* and *sarashina*) was established in 1870 and is now in the capable hands of fifth-generation owner Takeshi Muramatsu, who maintains the shop's policy of putting its all into each job, no matter how small or insignificant it may appear. The effort shows in the food and the service.

Because of the Great Kanto Earthquake in 1923 and extensive rebuilding in the area, the shop has been moved many times. It settled at the present location twenty-one years ago. A well-cared-for garden, easily viewed from the windows of the shop, makes for a relaxed environment right in the middle of the city.

Muromachi Sunaba became the soba-ya that it is at present soon after World War II. Before this it specialized in sweets, and as such it was very similar to the original confection makers credited with giving soba its delicate and refined nature (see History). Today, Muromachi Sunaba is so skillful at protecting the basics of soba cooking that even the critics and reviewers invariably leave satisfied.

Recommendations: Rolled Omelette (*Tamago-yaki*, ¥650) made fresh upon order and served hot is very popular, as are *Zaru* (¥650), Chicken Soba (¥1,300), and *Ten-mori* (¥1,400) and *Tenzaru* (¥1,500; the latter two have been served since 1950 in the original style).

How to get there: Walk down Chuo-dori toward Mitsukoshi Department Store. Turn right at Muromachi 4-chome Crossing. The shop is 50 yards down on the left.

Okina

2205 Nakamaru, Nagasaka-cho, Kita Koma-gun, Yamanashi Prefecture
☎ (0551) 32–5405
NEAREST STATION: Kobuchizawa Station, JR Chuo Hon Line
HOURS: 11:00–15:00, closed Mondays and Tuesday

Master Kunihiro Takahashi retired from the life of a company employee after only a short stint due to his uncompromising search for something to satisfy not only the pocketbook but also the soul. He trained with the legendary dissmeminator of the Issa-an style of soba, Yasuo Katakura, and then opened the Nagasaka Sarashina soba shop in Tokyo in 1974. The purity of his technique and the taste of the soba itself soon made his shop famous throughout Japan. With all this success, he was not satisfied. In 1987 he opened a new shop, away in the beautiful countryside of Nagasakacho, near the Shirakaba Museum. Here the only entrées on the menu are fresh (*Seiro*) and country-style (*Inaka Seiro*), both ¥820. Appetizers include only saké and freshly ground *wasabi* horseradish!

I visited on a snowy Sunday in February, but nevertheless, by one in the afternoon, this "cabin in the woods" soba shop, which seats 28, was bustling with sight-seeing couples, families, and individuals (coming by taxi) there to taste the real thing. If you are in the area (or just want a destination to shoot for on an outing from Tokyo), this shop is a must.

How to get there: From the station it is a 10-minute taxi ride toward Shirakaba Art Museum (Shirakaba Bijutsukan).

Tagoto Honten

12 Higashi Hairu, Sanjo-dori Teramachi, Nakagyo-ku, Kyoto
☎ (075) 221–3030
HOURS: 11:00–21:00

Established in 1925, this Kyoto restaurant keeps its traditional ways of making soba while searching for and developing new variations of on the standard 2:8 noodle. Most popular are the *sarashina* noodles (*Misogi Soba*, ¥1,000), Tempura Soba (¥1,000), and *Tagoto Soba* (hot noodles with *nori* and a mound of fresh abalone, all garnished with finely chopped scallions).

How to get there: Take a bus to the Kawaramachi Sanjo bus stop. Tagoto Honten is located in front of the famous Yata Jizo statue on the right.

Take Yabu

1144–2 Kashiwa, Kashiwa-shi, Chiba Prefecture
☎ (0471) 63–9838
NEAREST STATION: Kashiwa, JR Joban Line
HOURS: 11:45–20:00, closed Thursdays

After a twenty-year career operating the pace-setting shop of its time right next to the Sogo Department Store Mall in Kashiwa Station, Takeo Abe, 51, decided that he would dispense with the formalities associated with the restaurant business and open up his dream soba shop in the midst of nature, on top of a hill which has the freshest of breezes, 15 minutes from the station. I met Mr. Abe in the spring of 1980. It was at his first shop in the town that I had my initial encounter with "real soba." I had a cool dish of *Natto Soba*, then Tempura Soba, still sizzling and crackling as it was placed in front of me. Both portions were lean, as if to suggest, "What's your hurry? Why not have another fresh and delicious combination?"

Take Yabu, Kashiwa (near Tokyo)

The price of his food, even twenty years ago, was always a point of discussion, but he stuck to his guns, saying that only those who really loved soba should come to his shop. He was not making soba just to fill the stomach, but also to elevate the customer's appreciation of the simple things in life: soba was and is his medium and message.

One step into his new restaurant and you know you're in for a different kind of experience. Abe-san's keen natural sense, using the finest lacquer ware to serve his delicate portions of soba, lead many a student of the trade to visit and pick up a few hints.

As Kashiwa is a 30-minute train ride from Ueno, we're talking about a 3-to-4-hour outing, but it's a nice excuse to get out of the big city. The soba is of course of the best, but like the famous *yabu* shops, you need at least 2 or 3 portions to justify your journey. Yet this is the perfect setting for enjoying soba. Upon visiting this restaurant for the first time back in 1981, I was inspired to delve into the world of soba in earnest. Take Yabu has received wide acclaim as a leader and pacesetter of ever-expanding vision.

Favorite dishes: *Seiro Soba* (¥1,000), *Ten Seiro*, (¥2,400), and *Soba Kaiseki* (soba haute cuisine, ¥10,000).

How to get there: Turn right out the exit and go down the first set of stairs. You'll find a taxi stand nearby. Ask to be driven to Take Yabu. It's a quick 8 to 10 minutes from ¥800.

Yabu Soba

2–10 Kanda Awajicho, Chiyoda-ku, Tokyo
☎ (03) 3251–0287
NEAREST STATION: Awajicho Station, Marunouchi Line
HOURS: 11:30–19:00, closed Mondays

This restaurant is famous as the originator and sustainer of the *yabu* style, which goes back over one hundred years. It remains an ever-famous "in" spot of Tokyo.

Two fundamental trademarks found at all three of the *yabu* shops mentioned here refer to the noodle and the broth. The flour used to make the soba features the protein-rich, sweet-tasting outer part of the buckwheat to obtain a dark-brown, firm, and chewy country-style soba. This is combined with a strong blend of bonito stock, soy sauce, and *mirin*, sugar-blended and balanced in the traditional *yabu* way. This is the strong, stimulating dipping sauce of which the common laborers building the capital city of Tokyo during the Edo period (1600–1868) were so fond.

The portions are modest, so you will probably have to order extra large portions (*omori*) or even three trays of cooled soba (*seiro*) to be satisfied. (One tray costing ¥600 is referred to as *mori*, or you can pay ¥150 for having it covered with *nori*, a dish referred to as *Hanamaki Soba*). The *kaki-age* style of tempura (¥1,200), and in winter Wild Duck Soba (*Kamo-nanban Soba*, ¥1,500), are *yabu* standards whose popularity never fades. Also recommended is Soba Sushi (¥700). Even with the slim portions, customers always come back again and again. Maybe all Westerners should order large portions and consider it done with. If you go at peak hours, be prepared for a full house.

How to get there: Heading for Yushima-dori, walk 2 to 3 minutes down Sotobori-dori. You'll find the shop on Sotobori-dori just before the Kanda Post Office.

ADDITIONAL SHOPS

Ichiei

3–9–5 Higashi Ikebukuro, Toshima-ku, Tokyo
☎ (03) 3987–7051
NEAREST STATION: Ikebukuro, various lines
HOURS: 11:00–16:00, closed Sundays and holidays

How to get there: Exit the Seibu Department side of the station. Walk down Meiji-dori toward Kami Ikebukuro until you reach the five-cornered crossing (Tokyo Gas will be on the left). Pass under the highway and take the second street on your right. The shop is in the second block on the right.

Nanaki

1–13–2 Ebisu Nishi, Shibuya-ku, Tokyo
☎ (03) 3496–2878
NEAREST STATION: Ebisu Station, JR Yamanote Line or Hibiya Line
HOURS: 11:30–14:30, 17:00–21:30, closed Sundays and holidays

How to get there: Go out the main exit of Ebisu Station (on the Yamanote Line). Make a sharp right, cross the street, turn left, and then right at Wendys. The shop is across the street at the end of the block.

Shinano

2–10 Kagura-zaka, Shinjuku-ku, Tokyo
☎ (03) 3269–1411
NEAREST STATION: Iidabashi Station, JR Chuo Line
HOURS: 11:00–15:30, 17:00–20:30, closed Sundays and holidays

How to get there: Hand in your ticket at the exit nearest the Ichigaya side of the station and walk 5 minutes down the Kagurazaka Shopping Mall (*shoten-gai*). Turn right at Kinoben Confectionery. The shop is on your left.

Soba shop with rich wood interior ▶

Shinshu Sarashina

3–11–4 Moto Azabu, Minato-ku, Tokyo
☎ (03) 3403–3401
NEAREST STATION: Roppongi, Hibiya Line
HOURS: 11:30–20:30, closed Wednesdays

How to get there: Turn down the narrow street that runs alongside the Almond Coffee Shop toward the Ni-no-hashi Crossing. The shop is a 15-minute-walk, on the right one block before the crossing.

Sunaba

3–11–13 Toranomon, Minato-ku, Tokyo
☎ (03) 3431–1220
NEAREST STATION: Kamiyacho, Hibiya Line
HOURS: 11:00–14:00, 17:00–20:00, closed Sundays, Saturdays, and holidays

How to get there: Exit the stairwell leading to Fuji Bank (toward Toranomon). Walk down Sakurada-dori toward Toranomon. The shop is 5 minutes from the exit on the right side.

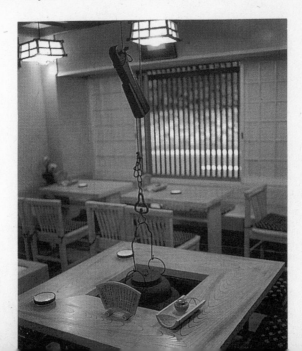

III

ABOUT SOBA

In the first year, I thought the taste of soba came from the skill of the cook.

In the second, I thought it came from the ingenuity and technique of the miller.

In the seventh year, I finally understood that the sweetness of soba is largely decided in the fields.

A field of buckwheat in bloom

In the act of lifting the soba from her bowl, a geisha pauses to gaze at a sparrow in flight (an *ukiyo-e* print ca. 1820–40, by Utagawa Toyokuni III)

Soba even found its way into Kabuki. Here the villain contemplates his next move over a bowl of "two-eight" noodles at a night stand (Utagawa Toyokuni III)

History

Buckwheat has always been a food for the people. In Eastern Europe it remains an essential staple in the daily diet and has held a respectable place in Western European cooking as well. Tracing the dissemination of buckwheat throughout the world and the subsequent development of a full-fledged soba cuisine in Japan has proved illuminating. Not only does it provide a fascinating look at the life and habits of an earlier time, it underscores buckwheat's vital role as an important food source as early as the fifteenth century in Europe and A.D. 800 in Japan.

The Dissemination of Buckwheat

There are many theories concerning buckwheat's name and place of origin. Modern-day crop evolution specialist Jack. R. Harlan, professor of plant genetics at the University of Illinois, Urbana, warns that "the idea of a center—an area in which things originate and out of which things are dispersed is reasonable, logical, and intellectually satisfying, but it does not always agree with the evidence." Harlan believes that "agriculture may originate in discrete centers or evolve over vast areas without definable centers." In other words, buckwheat may have evolved in several places simultaneously.

Nevertheless, as early as the end of the last century,

scientists had begun speculating on buckwheat's birth-place. The Swiss botanist Alphonse de Candolle, in his book *The Origins Of Cultivated Plants* (1881), maintained that it was near Lake Baikal or the valley-basin of the Amal River in Siberia, yet he cautioned that "it is hard to define the limit of the wild plant [the perennial species, *F. cymosum*, the probable ultimate source of both common and Tartary buckwheat] on (*sic*) the confines of Europe and Asia, in the Himalayas, because the nearer we approach its original country, the more often buckwheat escapes from cultivation and becomes quasi-wild. In Japan these semi-naturalizations are not rare." In the 1940s and 1950s other scientists placed the center of origin in the Manchurian region. Together, these ideas represent what is referred to as the Northern Theory.

The Southern Theory centering on China was proposed in the 1930s by the world-renowned Russian botanist, N. I. Vaviloff. Harlan wrote of the man and his work: "For nearly half a century the charisma of the man himself, and the elegant simplicity of his methodology have dominated theories and concepts about the origin of plants." In his "Botanical-Geographic Principles of Selection" (1935), Vaviloff stated that "the earliest and largest independent center of the world's agriculture and of the origin of cultivated plants consists of the mountainous region of central and western China, together with the adjacent lowlands." Included on his list of "Cereals And Other Grains" along with soybeans, adzuki beans, and millet were buckwheat (*F. esculentum moench*) and Tartar buckwheat (*F. tataricum gaertn*). But "in Vaviloff's time it was not possible to

Buckwheat's Probable Route

predict the enormous support that archaeology in general and archaeobotany in particular could give studies of the origin of cultivated plants and the emergence of agriculture. . . . The modern approach is more in the tradition of de Candolle than Vaviloff, in that attempts to integrate all sources of information" (Harlan). Yet, recent analysis of buckwheat seed remains excavated from sites in Hokkaido, Kyoto, and other areas has lent further credibility to the Southern Theory, and today it is the more widely accepted of the two. Specifically, the area of Unnan State in southern China is considered a likely candidate for buckwheat's origin.

Others have claimed that areas in and around Tibet and the Himalayan mountains of either Western China or Northern India were the site of buckwheat's beginnings.

Thomas Hunt, a professor of agronomy, wrote in 1914 that "although buckwheat is known to have been cultivated in China for 1,000 years (before coming to Europe), it is not believed to be very ancient, being 'unknown to the ancient Egyptians, Greeks and Romans.' The first written records are Chinese scripts of the fifth and sixth centuries."

From southern China, buckwheat is believed to have spread in all directions: westward to Nepal, northern India, and Bhutan; and north and east to the rest of China, Russia, and Korea.

Buckwheat came to Europe and America by traveling westward from its center of origin. De Candolle believed that the plant first entered Europe during the Middle Ages through Tatary and Russia. It probably passed through the lands of the Saracens, the nomadic Arabic peoples inhabiting the deserts between Syria and Arabia, for it later came to be widely known in French as *blé sarrasin* (Saracen wheat). Other opinions hold that returning crusaders brought back buckwheat from this area to Europe in the twelfth century. The *Oxford English Dictionary* (1933) states that "buckwheat was introduced into Europe by the Turks about the thirteenth century," while researchers Hughes and Henson (1934) mention it "reaching Germany early in the fifteenth century."

The earliest known reference to buckwheat's cultivation in Germany appeared in the Mecklenburgh register of 1436. It began to be widely cultivated in Russia during the 1400s, and during the 1500s it "spread toward the center of Europe and was cultivated for several centuries in England, France, Spain, Italy, Germany and Russia. It also found a place in the agriculture of Africa and Brazil" (Campbell). The earliest English language reference in the *Oxford English Dictionary* is by Turner in 1548.

Dutch colonists who settled along the Hudson River in what is now New York City brought buckwheat to America. In the 1800s it became popular in the South as an inexpensive flour source, and by 1866 an impressive 22 million bushels a year were being produced, primarily in New York and Pennsylvania. "Unlike the true cereal grains such as wheat, oats, and rye, it may be grown with abundant yields on poor, thin, arid soil where the climate is cool and moist" (Coe). The favorite use was in pancakes. This fare became so popular that it found its way into Stephen Foster's famous song "Oh, Susanna" of 1846:

> De buckwheat cake was in her mouth
> De tear was in her eye
> Says I: "I'm coming from de South"
> Susanna, don't you cry.

In fact, buckwheat cakes made from fresh flour even rated a mention in an 1882 magazine, *Garden*: "To go to America for a good . . . buckwheat cake" (OED).

Thereafter production began a long, slow decline. Several factors were responsible, including a decrease in the demand for buckwheat flour and for feed, the difficulty in developing new strains to improve crop yield, and advances in agricultural techniques that increased the yields of other crops on marginal farm land, nominally buckwheat's domain.

"In common with other countries, the acreage under buckwheat in Canada declined steadily until the early 1960s, but has increased since then as a result of demand for export, mainly to Japan. Since 1967, more than 50 percent of the total Canadian production has been centered in Manitoba. The yield per acre has fluctuated considerably, probably as a result of the susceptibility of the crop to such weather conditions as frost and drought. There has been no apparent increase in yield per acre in Manitoba over the last 25 years. Furthermore, Leighty has reported that over the period 1909–1913, the average yield in Canada was about 23–24 bushels per acre. Thus there appears to have been little or no increase in yield over the last 50 years and modern agricultural technology seems not so far to have made any significant impact on the crop" (De Jong).

Today, the Soviet Union and China are by far the world's leading producers of buckwheat, followed by France, Poland, Canada, and the United States.

Buckwheat Reaches Japan

Up until quite recently, with only scant references in historical documents to go by, scientists believed buckwheat to have entered southern Japan from Korea via the island of Tsushima around the first part of the seventh century.

With the development of more modern methods of investigation such as pollen analysis, however, historians have received new fuel for consideration. Utilizing this technique, scientists in Japan were able to analyze ancient buckwheat pollen found among excavated remains dating back to the Jomon period (10,000 B.C.– 300 B.C.) in the northernmost island of Hokkaido and in other areas of Japan as well. With discoveries like these, historians understandably differ as to exactly when and by which route buckwheat found its way to Japan.

Its earliest appearance in extant written records is not

a matter of conjecture, however. The word *buckwheat* first appears in historical documents dated 722, in one of six historical logs covering the period from 697 to 791, in the reign of the empress Gensho. It was a trying time, and the empress issued the following proclamation to local leaders: "It is now summer and there is no rain. Rice has been planted but is not growing. The possibility of famine looms. I command the officials to encourage the cultivation of buckwheat and barley and to set up warehouses in order to store the food harvested." Even then buckwheat's value as a quick-growing, highly nutritious food was understood, and monarchs relied on it in times when the more profitable rice crop failed them.

Known for its ability to grow even in barren soil and to go from seed to grain in the relatively short period of seventy-five days, buckwheat played an indispensable role as a crop that could help offset the effects of poor harvests and the dangers of famine. Due to primitive methods of cultivation, poor weather, and frequent states of war during these early times, rice was an extremely limited and precious commodity. Even when there was a decent harvest, the farmers were more inclined to use it as a form of payment of tax. Thus, buckwheat became a supplementary food along with wheat, millet, and barnyard grasses.

By the Kamakura period (1185–1333), buckwheat had become more widely available and is thought to have been eaten either as a whole grain in the form of gruels and porridges, or ground roughly into flour and used in a manner similar to wheat, millet, and other grains.

Gradually, cooking styles highlighting buckwheat's own unique character began to appear. Simple, filling foods like buckwheat dumplings developed. Variations on this dish sprang up across the country. Sweetened bean pastes or cooked vegetables such as pumpkins, turnips, and potatoes were stuffed into the centers of the dumplings. These were then steamed, baked, fried, or roasted to make primitive muffins and pastries.

Until the late sixteenth century, dumpling cooking in its numerous forms was the mainstay of buckwheat cooking. It is said that the shogun Hideyoshi Toyotomi, virtual ruler of Japan from 1588 to 1595 and a stout supporter of the tea ceremony, also had a great liking for the soba dumpling.

Just when and where soba noodles came into being is unclear, but hints can be gleaned from various documents, diaries, and other ancient literature. Generally,

A prototypical soba shop in the Shijogawara pleasure quarter of Kyoto. Note the long rolling pin still used by professional soba makers today. Artist unknown. *Nihonga*, ca. 1635.

THE BOOK OF SOBA

most Japanese culinary historians agree that soba noodles were probably first made in the confines of the temples and later spread to the general populace. This is a reasonable assumption since priests in those days traveled to China for training and in addition received guests from abroad.

The oldest extant writings mentioning buckwheat noodles, or *soba-kiri*, are said to be the diaries of the priest Jisho. In an entry dated February 3, 1614, he noted that "we were served buckwheat noodles at the Jomyo Temple" in Edo (Tokyo). In those days, only the wealthy people could afford to provide formal or decent burial grounds for their kin. As such, the less fortunate were often forced to abandon or bury their deceased in desolate mountain areas. Many of the common people would then pay their respects at local temples instead. At some point, Jomyo Temple priests began to offer temple guests a bowl of soba. Amusingly, and as so often happens, as word spread about the free service of these very satisfying noodles, people began to flock to this temple in large numbers. Eventually, the monks became annoyed at having to spend so much time meeting the demand and discontinued the service altogether.

Jisho's entry reveals no sense of surprise or novelty concerning the soba noodles. This suggests that they were no longer a new idea. So the question remains as to how far back the custom of soba noodles reaches. Since another work by the priest Genkei in the early Muromachi period (1394–1596) only mentions *udon* (thick wheat noodles) and *somen* noodles, the date can be approximated if not pinpointed. The modern-day buckwheat historian Shigeru Niijima places their development somewhere between 1596 and 1614.

The exact location of their origin is also open for debate. One book published in the Genroku period (1688–1704) cites the Seiun Temple (located near present-day Kofu, in Yamanashi Prefecture, 70 miles from central Tokyo), while another book, written about ten years later, gives the nod to the area around Kiso, Nagano Prefecture (previously Motoyama). Neither of these accounts claims to be indisputable, however, being only the result of hearsay. Furthermore, by modern standards, these two places are less than an hour's train ride apart.

In any event, it seems fair to assume that the techniques involved in making *udon* and *somen*, introduced from China to Japan during the Heian period (794–1185), eventually led to the development of soba noodles in Japan some four hundred years ago in the Yamanashi-Nagano region.

Some support for the above theory can be found in a light verse composed by a popular humorist of the Edo period (1600–1868) by the name of Shokusanjin (1749–1823). While visiting the popular resort area of Motoyama, he wrote the following play on words:

Everybody knows	*Motoyama no*
how famous Motoyama	*Soba meibutsu to*
is for buckwheat noodles	*Taremo shiru*
Here the luggage is	*Nimotsu wa koko ni*
put down/grated radish.	*Oroshi daikon.*

By tacking on the word *daikon* (radish) at the very end, he puns on the word *oroshi* (meaning both to "put something down" or "grate a vegetable"), changing the meaning from "Here the luggage is put down" to "Here the luggage is grated radish," a popular condiment for soba noodles.

The important point is simply that the area had already developed a reputation for its soba noodles, lending further credence to the Yamanashi-Nagano theory.

The Rise of Soba

During the years between 1596 and 1614, laborers and cooks poured in from all over the country to help with the development of the new capital city, Edo, under the new shogun, Ieyasu Tokugawa. It was during this time that soba noodles sprang into great popularity. In addition to being a food the laborers could afford, it provided a quick energy source both at lunchtime and at the end of a long, hard day. (Interestingly enough, just as in the pioneer days of the Wild West, three-quarters of the population in Tokyo was said to be male.) Also, soba noodles seemed to fit the personality of the people like a glove. This is clearly reflected by the following verse attributed to the famous haiku poet Basho (1644–1694): "Haiku and soba match the spirit of Tokyo."

In 1642, the government prohibited the selling of *udon*, soba, tofu, and similar nutritional staples for profit due to an extremely severe famine. Food was strictly rationed to each family, and meals had to be stretched by adding root plants to these basics.

In 1643, the first book describing the making of soba noodles in detail, *Tales of Cooking* (*Ryori monogatari*), was published. It mentions that buckwheat flour could be kneaded together with plain water, the water discarded during the washing of rice, hot water, or mashed tofu. That is, although taken for granted today, the practice of using wheat as a binding agent had not yet developed.

From the written evidence of several sources, the noodles at these early establishments were indeed made without the addition of wheat flour. Furthermore, it is thought that the noodles were most likely steamed instead of boiled. This technique was employed to compensate for the primitive methods of grinding that existed at the time. That is, since buckwheat has no gluten of its own and the flour produced back then was quite probably limited in its fineness and elasticity, noodles made from only buckwheat were prone to break into little pieces when boiled. (As buckwheat's protein melts and dissolves in hot water, there is not sufficient binding power to hold the noodles together.) By steaming, not only were the noodles not subjected to the rapid movement of boiling water, but what little elasticity the coarse flour did have could be coaxed out.

According to one theory, the idea of combining wheat and buckwheat flours is said to have been introduced by the Korean priest Genchin upon his visit to the famous temple Todaiji, sometime between 1624 and 1643. Yet, as other books published as late as 1689 fail to mention wheat as an ingredient in the process, it is thought that this did not become standard practice until at least the early 1700s, and perhaps not even until the mid-1720s. One cause for speculation is that, during this period, wheat was widely available only from late autumn to early spring.

In rural areas, such local sources as potatoes, burdock

leaves, and the young leaves of the buckwheat plant itself served as binding agents to help add strength and elasticity to the mixture. Even today, these variations on the basic soba noodle continue to be made.

In March 1657, as a result of the disastrous Furisode Fire, the economy of Tokyo suffered a severe setback. Over two-thirds of the city was destroyed in the two-day conflagrations, and more than 100,000 perished in it or the snowstorm that hit the city on the ensuing day.

Within four or five years, however, the city was reported to have been completely rebuilt, and in 1664 the government again permitted the selling of food (buckwheat noodles included) in public.

The book *Morisada Manko* (1853), a record of the customs of the Edo period, indirectly confirms the last point. The author wrote, "In 1664, *kendon* buckwheat noodles [explained below] appeared, but as yet were eaten only by the ordinary people, not being deemed fit for the noble classes." From this statement two things can be surmised. One, of course, is that the crucial period of adversity caused by famine and fire had subsided. The other is that, not only were the noodle dishes themselves of low quality, but the shops that sold them, set up to cater to the laborers and commoners, quite probably were centered in the "downtown" part of the city. Unlike the soba shops of today, the interiors were probably very sparse, functional affairs at best.

By taking a look at the names of two prototypical soba dishes (reported to have appeared as early as the period from 1624–1644), it becomes clear that in the early stages soba noodles appealed mainly to the lower classes. One dish, called "honest soba" (*shojiki soba*), was sold around the grounds of the Sensoji temple in Asakusa, and the other, "horseman's soba" (*umakatta soba*), was popular in the area around Denma Town in Yotsuya.

The first dish received its name from its close association with the temples, where honesty was the guiding rule of conduct. The latter was coined for people who had the taxing job of walking ahead of the horse and pulling its reins for the purpose of guiding aristocrats or delivering parcels to their proper destination. This was a popular means of getting from station to station during this period, and the horseman's service was in great demand. Walking long distances every day, their need for a good, cheap energy supply can easily be imagined. The area around Denma in Yotsuya became a regular stop along the route, a place where horsemen could "fuel up" by eating soba. They constituted such a steady clientele that the soba was named for them.

The reference to *kendon* soba in the earlier passage adds another dimension. The word *kendon* connotes a coarse or loud manner of speech or activity. During this period, the red-light district of Yoshiwara was in its initial stages. Various ranks of professional entertainers existed, according to their education and talent. Although extremely difficult to achieve, the highest rank conferred was that of *tayu*. This position was achieved only with great difficulty: women had to be proficient in poetry, the classics, calligraphy, and other arts, as well as be adept at the tea ceremony. Obviously, those who could qualify were so few in number that they could demand almost any price, and of course associated with only the very rich or those who had the same level of education. At the other end of the scale were those who had no education whatsoever. Virtually held hostage within the confines of their respective shops, they would call out to passersby in a loud voice, following this with no more than foolish chatter after services were rendered. Being at first loud, but later boring, they became known as "kendon girls."

In the same period, many soba shops offering only the cheapest and lowest-quality food also tried to draw customers to their shops by calling out in a loud voice. Once in the shop, however, the customers found the place totally lacking in etiquette: the shop's service came to an abrupt end when the customer's order was slapped down on the counter. Sure enough, their fare was soon tagged with the unbecoming name "kendon soba."

Soba Overtakes Udon

Before 1690, shops specializing in soba were rare. Generally, soba noodles were sold at *udon* restaurants and regular restaurants featuring rice dishes as a way to expand the menu, and at confectionery shops as an additional source of income.

Up until this time, *udon* was the mainstay of "Japanese pasta," and soba was still in its infancy. Eventually, however, shops specializing in soba came into their own and soon greatly outnumbered their predecessors. This situation is vividly depicted by the famous ukiyo-e artist Hishikawa Moronobu in his *Tokaido no bunken ezu* (*The Area Around Tokaido Station*) in 1690. Signboards for soba shops outnumber their *udon*/soba competitors 21 to six, and only one sign features *udon/somen*.

Central section of a humorous print of the 47 *ronin*. Three retainers eagerly devour bowls of soba, foreshadowing their final rendezvous in a soba shop. Hiroshige Ando. *Ukiyo-e* (detail), ca. 1830.

Soba shops were coming into their own, so much so that they began to appear in contemporary popular stories and legends. The year 1703 saw the culmination of the saga of the 47 *ronin*, or masterless samurai, one of the most celebrated incidents of perseverance and loyalty in Japanese history. On the night before the consummation of their two-year plan to revenge the wrongful treatment and consequent death of their lord, the 47 loyal retainers are said to have gathered on the second floor of a soba shop. Whether or not they actually met at a soba shop is questionable; yet the fact that stories and Kabuki plays written about this true tale portray it as being so at least indicates how pervasive soba shops had become.

Sometime between 1711 and 1726, the forerunner of today's *kake soba*, or Hot Soba Noodles in a Broth, is said to have appeared at the restaurant Shinano in Tokyo. Interestingly enough, unlike the hot version of today, it is reported that room-temperature or cool soup broth was poured over the cooked noodles. Laborers came in for a quick bowl of noodles and preferred to down them as quickly as possible. It can be imagined how waiting for the broth to be heated would have been a source of irritation. The expression "Arguments and fire are what Tokyo is known for" during this period accurately reflects the temperament of the times and certainly seems to lend credibility to this idea.

In 1728, an article published in a book dealing with the clothing, food, and daily life of the times stated that by 1726 the advertising board two-eight instant kendon soba had appeared in the Kanda area of Tokyo. That it was a variation of the basic kendon soba is certain, but what was the meaning of *two-eight* and *instant*?

Concerning the former, various explanations have been put forth, one being that *two-eight* signifies the ratio of wheat to buckwheat flour (that is, two parts wheat to eight parts buckwheat). Another possibility concerns the price of the soba itself. The currency of the time was *mon* instead of the yen of today. Therefore, the term *two-eight* is thought to have stood for two portions of soba at eight mon each, a price considered to be well within the means of the laborers. Both of these interpretations, as well as others, are still a matter of speculation today.

The word *instant* in the signboard is worth a bit more reflection. If allowed to sit for a while after rolling out and cutting, soba made from 100-percent buckwheat is prone to dry up and hence break into small pieces when cooked, even if it is carefully steamed. To prevent this from happening, the noodles are rolled and cut fresh upon order, obviously requiring the customer to wait. Thus, the concept of "instant" soba would not have been possible. However, if wheat is added to the process the noodle will hold together, due to the wheat's gluten. Accordingly, soba noodles can be made in advance, "cooked instantly" or even precooked, and simply reheated, as many of today's fast-food noodle stands do. This, then, is thought to be the real significance of the two-eight instant kendon soba signboard. The technique of blending wheat flour with the buckwheat had finally become a standard practice.

The Emergence of a Soba Cuisine

Edo-period culture reached its peak during the years 1751 to 1801. Gradually, the increased level of extravagance started to create a period of decadence, said to have occurred between 1804 and 1830. Soba shops were greatly affected.

Originally considered a food for the working class, soba cuisine slowly evolved in more sophisticated establishments

Humorous depiction of farmers celebrating a successful harvest with soba.

that were now frequently visited by the aristocrats.

From around 1789, the shops started to be redecorated with gorgeous *tatami* interiors resembling those of elegant teahouses, and began to offer saké. Also at about this time, the restaurant Nagasaka, located in Azabu near Roppongi, started to feature the highly refined pure-white—and subsequently different-colored and -flavored—buckwheat noodles, in addition to the standard type.

Utensils became more refined as well. Exquisitely

worked soba utensils—serving trays, porcelain, and so on—appeared which, if made today, would demand phenomenal prices. One of the most representative pieces of the era is the *Lacquered Kendon Box* owned for a time by the writer Takizawa Bakin. Considered a masterpiece of craftsmanship, it is an exquisitely lacquered black box with a shiny shell-type design painted on the outside. More than just your average container, it made a great impression on the lords and aristocrats visiting the soba establishments where it was displayed. It is recorded that this piece was part of an antique exhibition during the early 1800s. Even today, it can be seen at museums exhibiting the works of the Edo period.

By 1818, there were said to have been over 6,000 noodle shops, about half of them soba shops. It was reported that you couldn't walk more than 150 yards in any direction without running into at least one soba shop.

In direct contrast to the growing sophistication of the high-class restaurants, the low-class shops, now commonly referred to as "two-eight" shops, sank even lower. Eventually this earned them the reputation of serving "junk-food" soba (*da-soba*). To distinguish their establishments further from lesser shops, the masters of the better shops began to post signs such as handmade (*te-uchi*) or one-hundred-percent soba (*ki-soba*) in front of their shops. Imagine the wit of putting out a sign reading handmade in an age when noodle machines had not yet come into being. Of course, everything was still being made by hand, but the intended meaning was "We are selling soba that is skillfully made from high-quality ingredients—not junk food."

Near the end of the Edo period, the two-eight shops

began to imitate the high-class shops by upgrading their decor and exteriors. Some even went so far as to put out the same handmade signs in front of their stores. Gradually it became difficult to distinguish one from the other, thus marking the beginning of the situation that exists today. Unless tipped off and led to such a shop by a friend, it became impossible to detect from the outside which shop was really serving high-quality, handmade soba.

According to the previously mentioned book *Morisada Manko*, around 1860 there was an official meeting of soba-shop proprietors concerning the standardizing of prices. Over 3,700 soba shops were on the register for this meeting although the actual number of shops must have been far greater. Today, although the population of Tokyo is more than ten times what it was during the late Edo period, the number of soba shops has only doubled.

Nighthawk, Wind-Chime, and Night-Stand Soba

In the evenings Edo's street stalls began to sell hot soba noodles in a hearty broth meant to cut the chill. It is not clear when they first began, but as a perusal of old government notices reveals that they were temporarily prohibited in 1686 due to the outbreak of numerous fires (a result of careless operators), it is evident that they existed before that time.

As the hawk is also active late into the night, the nickname *yotaka-soba* ("nighthawk soba") was soon appended to the stalls. Another contributing factor is said to have been that these establishments were often frequented by streetwalkers out looking for customers.

Although this kind of activity was officially restricted to the confines of Yoshiwara, there were those who dared to solicit elsewhere. Upon calling out to a potential customer, they would say "*Chotto, chotto*" ("Just a minute. . . ."), which somewhat resembled the hawk's cry, "cho, cho." True or not, the nickname stuck. In any event, both the nighttime stall operators and the street professionals received the nickname "nighthawk" for their nocturnal habits.

A short lyric-like verse (*senryu*) penned around this period plays on, among other things, these two nighthawks.

> Two customers
> woman's work done
> brings three helpings of soba.

> *Kyaku futatsu*
> *Tsuhushite yotaka*
> *Mitsu kui.*

Two nighthawkers. A kabuki scene. Utagawa Toyokuni I. *Ukiyo-e*, ca. 1816.

THE BOOK OF SOBA

The shogunate's control over Edo and the rest of Japan began to decline toward the end of the Edo period. Where once strict punishment was meted out for any critical stance taken toward the ruling class, near the end indirect ridicule became the order of the day. In this print a samurai falls victim to a dog and a tray of soba. Utagawa Hirokage. *Ukiyo-e* (detail), 1859.

Both in Tokyo and Osaka, respectable people began visiting these stands. They were known to approach inconspicuously and order in a soft voice. While it is probably true that they didn't want to disturb or awaken the neighborhood people (who lived in dwellings literally constructed of thin wood and paper walls and who, in addition, customarily rose and set with the sun, due to the expense of oil lighting and heating), it is not unreasonable to assume that they wanted to avoid any association with the seedier aspects of the business.

In order to encourage well-heeled visitors and keep up to date with their *udon* cousins, soba operators in Tokyo began to upgrade their stalls. They struck upon the idea of using the delicate sound of a wind chime to lure customers. Other inducements, including charming bowls and a wide selection of choice garnishes, were added as well. Appropriately enough, these stalls became known as "wind-chime soba" stands and became a tremendous hit.

Not to be outdone by the success of their rivals, the night-hawk sellers also started to attach wind chimes to their stands. In response, the original wind-chime stands began calling out to the customers. Once again, it became virtually impossible to distinguish between the styles.

From 1804 to 1830, the number of soba shops offering good quality fare at reasonable prices began to increase. As a result of this and the extravagance of the age, the image and popularity of the night stands began to wane. Gradually they were by and large forced out of business.

Soba from 1868 to the Present

The buckwheat available in Tokyo during the Meiji period (1868–1912) came primarily by one of two routes: what are known as the mountain route and the river route. Buckwheat from the former was transported by horse from the mountainous areas of Nerima and Jindaiji, northwest of Tokyo, or from the Fujisawa area, southwest of Tokyo. Ground mainly in the Shinjuku and Hodogaya areas, the flour was then distributed among the stores of Tokyo. The Ishimori flour factory in Nakano (near Shinjuku) and the Kitagawa flour factory in Hodogawa trace their roots back to this period.

However, with the moving of the imperial capital to Tokyo, this supply became insufficient. Increasingly larger quantities of buckwheat were shipped in from country areas to satisfy demand. Unfortunately, after undergoing such long storage under moist conditions, this buckwheat's quality was thought to be considerably inferior.

In the early stages, the buckwheat was turned into flour utilizing man-powered stone grinders 21 inches (one *chokei*) in width. At about the time of the war between Japan and China in 1894–95, oil engines began to be employed. Nowadays, mainly steel roll grinders from Europe are used, in addition to the few stone grinders still employed to provide high-quality flour to traditional "handmade" shops.

In March 1888, with the first patenting of a noodle machine, by a Mr. Shinzaki from the Kyushu region, the long road from handmade to machine-made noodles was bridged.

In 1942, amid World War II, the whole Japanese economy collapsed and, along with the other industries, the restaurant business was completely abandoned. Finally, in 1950, the economy began to recover and the restaurant industry reestablished itself. It is said that the supply of food in Japan was critical during the war years but actually worse during the six years that followed. Due to the scope of their defeat, it is perhaps unavoidable that Japan's attention shifted from things Japanese to Western styles. As a result, not only did the ingredients and techniques of the soba maker suffer a temporary decline in quality, but the consciousness of the people concerning soba's place in the daily diet seemed to have received a mighty blow as well.

With the passage of 40 years, over 40,000 soba shops have sprung back up over the country. But 80 to 90 percent of these retain only the most superficial resemblance to real soba establishments, content to serve buckwheat noodles that in reality contain as much wheat as they do buckwheat. In all fairness, these can be refreshing and enjoyable. Yet, if the public's conception of buckwheat stops at this level of awareness, an injustice is being done to this, nutritious and tasty food.

Nowadays, the word *soba* is lumped together along with spaghetti, *udon*, etc., as just another type of noodle. In fact, if you mention the word *soba* to people under 30, they are likely to think you are referring to *ramen* (Chinese noodles). Yet a resurgent breed carries on with the traditional techniques, serving up buckwheat noodles worthy of their name. However, if you are not led by a friend to one of these establishments, you probably will not have the pleasure of tasting the real thing. Hopefully, the list of shops at the end of this book will help to bridge this gap.

At the same time, Japan now produces only 20 percent of the buckwheat it consumes, with the largest supplier being China, followed by Canada, the United States, and Brazil. Wouldn't it be nice if people in the West could pick up the slack, become more aware of the nugget of nutrition that their countries have in abundance, and give life back to buckwheat noodles?

Nutrition

Soba noodles provide the best of two worlds. First, they are a quick source of high-quality nutrition and boast a superior protein makeup, along with an abundance of vitamin B1, vitamin P (with the valuable flavonoid rutin known for its effectiveness in reducing the cholesterol count in the blood), and dietary fiber. Secondly, while the word *pasta* connotes calorie and weight gain in the minds of many people, soba noodles are virtually fat-free. Consuming one large portion (7 ounces) of noodles per day plus a piece of fresh fruit or salad provides an abundance of usable high-quality protein and close to 40 percent of the adult recommended daily amount of vitamin B. It is no wonder that for centuries soba has been a popular traditional item of Japanese cuisine.

Buckwheat's nutritional and medicinal value was realized long before the twentieth century. One of the earliest known nutritional/folk-medicinal references concerning buckwheat in Japan, the *Honcho shoku kan* (*Food Dictionary*), published in 1697, reads: "Buckwheat is sweet, contains no poison, relaxes the nerves, eases irritability, and helps to clear out and release old feces from the stomach and intestines."

In a modern work of the same nature, *Kampo shokumotsu seishitsu to koyo* (*Herbs and Food*

Character and Effectiveness), the text is even more specific: "Soba is a very nourishing food which works to relax the body; helps relieve and prevent inflammation, excessive perspiration, nosebleed, or high blood pressure; and helps maintain a good functioning of the intestine by working to remove old feces from the intestines."

Interestingly enough, one of today's top soba historians and authors, Shigeru Niijima, notes that the popular Japanese custom of eating buckwheat on the last day of the year (*Toshikoshi Soba*), which continues to this day, served a dual purpose. Not only did the quick, fortifying meal give merchants and others with busy year-end schedules a burst of needed energy to complete their last-minute chores, they also benefited from buckwheat's cleansing of the digestive tract. That is, buckwheat helped them to start the New Year off with a clean slate physically as well as mentally.

The custom of eating buckwheat on the last day of the year can be traced all the way back to the Kamakura period (1185–1333), long before the advent of soba noodles "just" four hundred years ago. Originally, buckwheat was made into dumplings and used as a portable food for ninja and ascetics who spent extended periods of time training or traveling in remote mountain areas. Having very few or no sophisticated cooking utensils available, they would cook dumplings and carry them for the next few days' meals. In emergencies or when no cooking utensils were available at all, they would dissolve buckwheat flour in water and drink it. As buckwheat requires little cooking, keeps well, can even be reheated, and most importantly was found to contain enough nutrition to sustain a traveler through his rigors, it was ideal for these times of austerity when stamina was a must.

One of the most intriguing accounts of Japan's traditional reliance on buckwheat was given at The Second International Buckwheat Symposium held in Kyushu, Japan, in 1983. Presented by the Reverend Shocho Hagami of the Mt. Hiei Buddhist sanctuary, the account links buckwheat with the demanding practice of *kaihogyo*, a Buddhist rite.

Mt. Hiei and Buckwheat

About twelve hundred years ago when Kyoto was the political and cultural center of Japan, the master priest Dengyo Saicho set up a sanctuary on Mt. Hiei and erected the Enryaku-ji temple, establishing the home of the Tendai sect of Buddhism. In A.D. 766, at the age of 19, he climbed deep into the forests of the mountain, built a thatched hut, and began a life of meditation and discipline. At 38 he undertook a voyage to China. China at that time was a formidable power and a great cultural center in the East. Saicho studied there for only six months but returned to Japan with a rich knowledge of esoteric teachings, Zen doctrines, and many other precepts, including the orthodox Tendai philosophy.

Soon after his return, Saicho set up the Tendai sect at Mt. Hiei, which was to become one of the pillars of Japanese Buddhism. Almost concurrently he became the first priest to be given the title of master by the imperial court.

The Mt. Hiei sanctuary is well known for its austere disciplines. The most austere are walking training (*kaiho-gyo*), burning-of-wooden-sticks training (*goma-gyo*), and seclusion training (*rozan-gyo*). The latter was established by Saicho and has been transmitted down to the present day over eleven centuries. For a period of twelve years of seclusion in the mountains, a priest in *rozan-gyo* devotes himself to the service of Buddha, dressing in simple robes and living on a frugal diet; he observes almost unbearably strict commandments and daily exercises in an inclement environment, often at the risk of his life.

Kaiho-gyo is a discipline to be observed in prayer for the attainment of higher spiritual powers as described in a chapter of the Lotus Sutra. It entails a strict discipline requiring the priest to walk the peaks and glens to visit many places of worship over the course of 1,000 days. These days of self-discipline are divided into ten segments of 100 days each, and it takes seven years to complete the ten rounds. The first three years may be called the preparation period, when only one round of 100 days of 18-plus miles a day is allowed. Making two rounds a year is compulsory in the fourth and fifth year, which adds up to 700 days in five years. Up until the seven-hundredth day a priest is supposed to walk up and down 18 miles every day, chant sutras, and perform other rituals at the 300-odd pre-designated spots, including temples and historic ruins. Immediately after the seven-hundredth day the priest confines him in the Meio-do temple for nine days, where he chants a set prayer 100,000 times without eating any food, without drinking a drop of water, and without lying down to rest or sleeping a wink. This is the preliminary *goma-gyo*. In the eighth round of walking, the distance to be covered in one day is doubled, with an additional discipline of walking up and down the steep Kihara slope to the Sekizan temple (a temple at the western foot of Mt. Hiei) and back. In the ninth round the distance is extended to 52 miles. During the 100 days of the final round the walking is reduced to the original distance of 18 miles.

After the successful completion of this 1,000-day discipline, buckwheat comes to the fore. To purify himself for the final training—one last round of *goma-gyo*—the priest must first undertake a 100-day fast called *gokoku-dachi*. *Gokoku* refers to five basic cereals: rice, barley, wheat, soybean, and adzuki beans; *-dachi* means abstinence. The priest is not to ingest any grains, nor is he allowed to take salt. Since eating any kind of animal food is prohibited in Buddhism, he eats no staple food that is considered necessary for subsistence from the viewpoint of modern nutritional science. *But there is one exception to the rules: he is allowed to eat buckwheat.*

Certainly, hundreds of years of folk knowledge and remedies played a part in selecting buckwheat for its role in *gokoku-dachi*. Another factor may have been buckwheat's ability to grow and even flourish at higher altitudes. Mt. Hiei's elevation (2,750 feet) makes it an almost ideal place for cultivating the grain. In any case, buckwheat had already proven itself many times before the Reverend Hagami began *kaiho-gyo* at the age of 45 in 1947 and completed *goma-gyo* at 51 in 1953. Even at the ripe age of 81 he remained confident that the centuries-old training speaks for itself, as he concluded, "I dare to say that the process is absolutely rational and scientific."

Although successful completion of this training depends mainly on the daily effort and courage of the disciple, modern research on the subject of buckwheat supplies an abundance of convincing evidence to affirm its nutritional value. I want to add here that in compiling the following report I am indebted for much of the information to Dr. Keisuke Tsuji of the National Institute of Nutrition (Japan); Ivan Kreft and Branka Javornik of the University of Ljubljana (Slovenia); and Bjorn Eggum of the National Institute of Animal Science (Denmark).

Protein and Amino Acids

Among buckwheat's many fine qualities, perhaps its excellent amino-acid composition stands out above the rest. Of the twenty or more amino acids needed for the human body to function properly, eight to ten are termed "essential amino acids," as they cannot be synthesized or produced by our bodies and so must be obtained from our daily food. A food's value as a protein source depends not just on the total amount of protein it has, but also on the amount of protein the body can use. This amount is referred to as the Net Protein Utilization, or NPU.

From the specialist's point of view, eggs are considered to be an almost perfect protein food. That is, eggs contain all of the essential amino acids in the highest and most well-balanced proportions and have an NPU of 94. By comparison, buckwheat is ranked at 74, wheat germ 67, beef 67, chicken 65, soybeans 61, and wheat 47 (Fig. 1).

Although animal foods (including dairy products) occupy the upper rankings, they also carry with them

Food	Npu (percentage)	Food	Npu (percentage)
Eggs	94%	Hamburger	67%
Park	82	Oatmeal	66
Fish	80	Tofu	65
Cottage cheese	75	Chicken	65
Buckwheat flour	74	Soybeans, soy flour	61
Brown rice	70	Wheat flour	47
Cheese	70	Peanuts	43
Wheat germ	67	Lentils	30
Beef (steak)	67		

Fig. 1. Net Protein Utilization Scores

high levels of fat and cholesterol. Buckwheat's score of 74 indicates that the body can utilize all but 26 percent of the available protein. This score, though respectable for a grain, does not reflect the fact that 17 percent of the undigestible substance is high-crude fiber, which is only now receiving attention for its essential role in the human diet (see Dietary Fiber).

A breakdown of the protein by amino acids (Fig. 2) reveals that buckwheat contains high amounts of lysine. Lysine is important for its ability to help the body utilize and convert protein. It is often present in only small amounts in plant protein. Bjorn Eggum acknowledges the role that foods high in lysine play when combined with grain, for example:

> It is a general assumption that the quality of animal protein is better than protein of plant origin. This is a very general statement as several vegetable proteins, e.g., protein from buckwheat, can be of very high quality. However, it is true that animal proteins in most cases have a high lysine content. Furthermore, the digestibility of animal products is in general very high.

Fig. 2. Protein Quality in Grains and Animal Foods

Amino Acid	GRAINS					ANIMAL PRODUCTS			
	Buckwheat (g/16gN)	Barley (g/16gN)	Wheat (g/16gN)	Rye (g/16gN)	Maize (g/16gN)	Egg (g/16gN)	Meat and bone scraps (g/16gN)	Pork (g/16gN)	Fishmeal (g/16gN)
	43.26	41.16	36.03	38.03	42.45	56.73	49.56	46.88	33.85
Lysine (1, 5)	5.09	3.69	2.55	3.68	2.76	6.79	7.93	7.99	4.82
Arginine (1, 1)	8.85	5.38	4.62	5.68	4.35	6.19	5.79	5.88	7.26
Tryptophan (1, 1)	1.59	1.11	1.03	1.16	0.62	1.48	1.00	1.38	0.82
Methionine (2, 5)	1.89	1.82	1.81	1.74	2.37	3.09	2.78	2.85	1.21
Valine (3, 7)	4.69	5.33	4.50	4.60	5.00	7.58	5.75	4.76	3.76
Isoleucine (3, 6)	3.48	3.68	3.39	3.15	3.78	5.78	4.80	4.39	2.54
Cystine (3, 4)	2.02	2.30	1.79	1.99	2.24	2.38	1.00	1.14	0.58
Leucine (4, 7)	6.11	7.11	6.82	5.96	10.51	8.94	7.99	7.25	5.21
Threonine (4, 8)	3.15	3.60	2.84	3.33	3.88	5.17	5.04	4.28	2.88
Phenylalanine (5, 8)	4.19	4.91	4.38	4.41	4.53	6.71	5.19	3.88	3.08
Histidine (5, 8)	2.20	2.23	2.30	2.33	2.41	2.62	2.29	3.08	1.69

NOTE: The first set of figures in parentheses ranks buckwheat's amino acid against those of the listed grains. The second set of figures indicates buckwheat's ranking inclusive of the protein-rich animal products. SOURCE: Eggum, "The Protein Quality of Buckwheat in Comparison with Other Protein Sources of Plant or Animal Origin." (1980)

. . . animal proteins have a high lysine content and will as such have a positive complementary effect on protein quality in diets based on cereals.

Buckwheat's protein works in the same way. When wheat is combined with buckwheat, as in the noodle-making process (wheat acts as a binding agent), the soba noodle attains an NPU of 81 percent due to the high lysine content. By combining soba, wheat, and soybeans (see Soy-Soba Noodles, page 90), an NPU rivaling that of eggs is possible. (Fig. 2)

Allowing for small fluctuations due to the variety of the plant and the growing conditions, "the concentration of lysine in buckwheat is almost always above 5 percent, reaching the ideal level of lysine in proteins proposed by FAO/WHO group" (Kreft). This is roughly twice the amount of lysine in either wheat or white rice.

Compared with brown and well-milled white rice, buckwheat noodles (with 35 percent wheat) contain 9.7 percent protein by weight (brown rice contains 7.4 percent and white rice 6.8 percent), or roughly 1.5 times the protein found in white rice. When cooked, the figures are 4.8 percent, 3.3 percent, and 2.6 percent respectively. This difference is considerable. Buckwheat groats and dumplings score even higher.

Vitamin P and Rutin

When we think about the important vitamins present in buckwheat, vitamin P, containing the valuable flavonoid rutin, stands out as one of buckwheat's most important characteristics. In Japan and China, it is common knowledge that buckwheat is an effective preventative measure against high blood pressure. This is due to the rutin present in buckwheat but absent in other grains.

Rutin is known to keep the capillaries and arteries strong and flexible, protecting the body against the internal and external bleeding and hemorrhages which may accompany old age. It also protects the blood vessels from rupturing or forming clots.

Today, medicine containing rutin together with vitamin C is used to treat high blood pressure, arteriosclerosis, and purpura (a seepage of blood into the skin and mucous membranes that causes purplish discoloration). Thus, by combining buckwheat with foods high in vitamin C (which buckwheat lacks), the effectiveness of the rutin in buckwheat is strengthened.

Buckwheat flour in its raw state contains about 6.5 mg of rutin per 100 g. Although the amount of rutin remains constant regardless of growing conditions, it decreases slightly when exposed to heat and light. Boiled buckwheat contains 1.2 mg of rutin per 100 g. Rutin, like vitamins B1 and B2, dissolves easily in water. Fortunately, in the case of soba noodles, the cooking water, or *soba-yu*, is served to the customer near the end of the meal. To receive the full benefit of the nutrition contained in buckwheat noodles, it is essential to drink this cooking water to close off a meal. Combined with a little of the leftover soup broth, this provides a most satisfying sweet taste while aiding in digestion.

Vitamins B1 and B2

In addition to vitamin P, buckwheat contains considerable amounts of vitamins B1 and B2. The former plays an important role in rekindling energy by facilitating the working of the nerves. It is also effective in cases of exhaustion, irritability, and loss of appetite. Vitamin B2 assists the lipids in their work (see below). If taken together with vitamin E, it becomes an effective precaution against hardening of the arteries (arteriosclerosis).

Cooked soba noodles have about two times more vitamin B1 than cooked white rice. If we mix hot water into buckwheat flour and beat it into the form of dumplings, thereby eating buckwheat without losing any of its valuable water-soluble elements (including B1) during the boiling process, we can provide 40 percent of the adult recommended daily amount of vitamin B1 by eating only 100 grams (or about one-quarter of a pound) of buckwheat.

Kazuo Fujimura mentions in the nutrition chapter of his book *Soba Technique* that during the Edo period, beriberi was prevalent in Japan. At the time, the people of Tokyo were terrified of the disease. Though they didn't know its cause, they somehow knew enough to eat soba noodles, which they did often and with a passion. Fittingly, they earned the label "soba crazy" from outsiders.

Vitamin B2 occurs in buckwheat flour in an amount only about one-fourth that of B1 (0.11 mg B2 per 100 g buckwheat flour, as opposed to 0.46 mg B1). Yet that is almost twice the amount in brown rice (0.6 mg) and four times that of white rice (0.3 mg).

Dietary Fiber

Dietary fiber is a carbohydrate that is not easily assimilated or digested; yet it is now being recognized as playing an essential role in the prevention of many adult diseases afflicting Western countries. Dr. Dennis Burkitt, a surgeon and epidemiologist on the British Medical Research Council, is credited with starting this new trend of thought. Two decades of study and work in a hospital in Africa, where the diet is high in fiber, led him to the conclusion that an intestinal disorder known as diverticulosis is caused by a diet consisting of too many refined carbohydrates. In 1972 he supported his earlier findings with another study stating that a decrease in dietary fiber in the diet corresponds to high incidences of cardiovascular disease, appendicitis, gallbladder disease, hernia, and colon cancer.

At Chiba University in Japan, several experiments have been carried out on rats to see what effect, if any, the addition of buckwheat to the diet may have on the cholesterol in the blood. In one experiment, a group of rats (Group A) was fed a diet of 55 percent raw buckwheat and other nutrients that were kept constant for both groups. The rats in Group B were given a diet consisting of 55 percent raw wheat. (All other factors remained the same.) In an analogous test, cooked soba noodles (made from 45 percent buckwheat and 55 percent wheat) were substituted for the raw buckwheat in Group A, and cooked *hiya-mugi* (a noodle made only from wheat) was substituted for the raw wheat in Group B. In both experiments, it was reported that Group A— the group fed buckwheat—recorded considerably lower levels of cholesterol in the blood and an increase in the proportion of cholesterol with a high concentration of lipoproteins. From the specialist's point of view, cholesterol is known to have either low (often very low) or high amounts of lipoproteins. While the types of cholesterol with low lipoprotein levels are carried over into the cells of the blood vessels (known to be a main factor in cases of cerebral hemorrhaging and heart attacks), the type of cholesterol with a high density of lipoproteins is removed from the cell membranes.

Fiber reduces serum cholesterol and neutral fat because fiber increases bile discharge to the intestine at the same time that cholesterol is discharged. Cardiovascular and cerebrovascular diseases are caused by cholesterol and/or neutral fat deposits inside the blood vessels. Therefore the incidence of heart disease in rural Africa is relatively low, since people there have less cholesterol and fat in their blood.

Such research is still being conducted, and buckwheat continues to make a strong showing. Further studies that will help us to eat better and provide protective measures against such adult diseases as high blood pressure, diabetes, and cerebral hemorrhaging are eagerly awaited.

Lipids

By now it has become evident that buckwheat, among other things, helps the body eliminate unwanted cholesterol. As a footnote to the above discussion, a look at the lipids in buckwheat is appropriate.

Buckwheat contains 2 to 3 percent lipids, which are distributed mainly within the embryo and secondarily within the endosperm. Close to 30 percent of these lipids (also known as fatty acids) are made up of the valuable and main essential fatty acid, linoleic acid. Nutritionally speaking, linoleic acid is known to help decrease blood cholesterol levels and provide protection against the coagulation of blood within the blood vessels. In addition, it has a low level of free fatty acid, which means that it does not change or putrify even if stored for a long period.

The lipids in buckwheat contain abundant amounts of physiologically effective plant sterol (0.2 percent). This percentage is largely made up of sitosterol, stigmasterol, and campesterol. The main physiological effects of these sterols are to prevent cholesterol from increasing in the blood serum, as well as to absorb cholesterol within the small intestine.

Minerals

Potassium, magnesium, phosphate, and iron are abundantly present in buckwheat flour (especially in grades 2 and 3 of Japanese flour). Generally speaking, soybeans and other beans are noted for their potassium and magnesium content, another demonstration of buckwheat's resemblance to the bean family. Of special interest is that buckwheat contains more iron than other grains. These minerals play an essential role in the prevention of hypertension and anemia.

Another effective element within buckwheat is colin, which facilitates the working of the liver. Although excessive drinking places a burden on the liver, drinking on occasion and within reason is one of life's pleasures. Depending on how much and how often one drinks, of course, colin will to some extent assist in preventing excess fat from collecting in the liver (that is, assist in the prevention of fatty-acid buildup, a problem for people who consume too much alcohol). In addition, the methionine and niacin in buckwheat also work to help the liver. It is not only in jest that soba is said to be an ally of the habitual drinker.

Buckwheat and Other Foods

By combining small amounts of egg, tempura, chicken, or vegetables with a bowl of soba noodles and then garnishing with the mineral-rich condiments that accompany soba cuisine, a nutritional meal that approaches the ideal balance of nutrients can be made. In addition to the traditional hot and cold soba noodles, the variety of other dishes—the soba dumpling, buckwheat cookies and crackers, and soba sushi—provide us with a wealth of menu ideas to enjoy.

In both the United States and Japan the Chinese-style *ramen* noodle is becoming increasingly popular, even though it has nowhere near soba's nutrients and versatility.

By adding the ever-adaptable buckwheat to Western or even Chinese cooking, this traditional food could capture the fancy and recognition of young and old alike. Dr. Tsuji put it best when he said that he hoped "buckwheat would graduate from its position in the hands of the soba professional to reach its deserved status as a food valued and used by all for its nutrition and inherent sweet taste."

Whole seed, flour, and dried noodles

Buckwheat: From Seed to Table

Common buckwheat (*Fagopyrum esculentum*), the main character in this book, is one of about fifteen species within the genus *Fagopyrum*. The name comes from the Latin *fagus*, "beech," and the Greek *pyros*, "wheat," and alludes to the seeds being shaped like those of beech trees, or beech-mast, whence their name derived from the German *buchweizen*, "beechwheat." This genus belongs to the family of Polygonaceae "which includes various species of sorrel and dock (*rumex*), and of smartweed, knotweed, bindweed (*polygonum*), all more or less troublesome weeds" (Hunt). Quite clearly, buckwheat is a different breed of plant than the normal cereal grains of rice, wheat, millet, rye, and oats, which all belong to the family of Gramineae.

There are two principal varieties of common buckwheat (*F. esculentum*) grown in the United States and Canada, silverhull and Japanese, from which a great majority of the buckwheat groats and flour products come (Coe). These, and similar varieties are cultivated mainly in China, Russia, Canada, the United States, Nepal, India, Japan, and Korea, and are also a crop of some importance in Yugoslavia, Poland, Hungary, Brazil, South Africa, and other African countries. More recently, these have been cultivated in Austria, Switzerland, Italy, France, Great Britain, and Australia.

Able to grow within the unusually short span of 75 days, buckwheat is easily cultivated twice a year: "summer" buckwheat (planted in late May or early June, harvested in August) and "autumn" buckwheat (planted in late July or early August, harvested in October). In general the latter variety is known to have superior taste and fragrance due to the cooler temperatures at night. By and large, autumn buckwheat is the variety which makes its way to the shelves of our supermarkets and health-food stores.

The second variety, *F. tataricum*, referred to variously as "Tartary buckwheat," "Indian wheat," or "rye buckwheat," "is grown to a limited extent in the mountains of North Carolina, in Maine, in New York, and in a number of other places in the United States and Canada, as well as being reported as growing in the Himalayas of northeastern India and China under cooler and harsher climatic conditions, to which it is better adapted than common buckwheat" (Coe). As its nickname "bitter buckwheat" implies, its taste and milling qualities do not compare favorably with the common varieties. In addition to possessing this slightly unbecoming characteristic, it can be clearly distinguished from common buckwheat in a number of ways. The seed is not as angular as that of common buckwheat, and at a quick glance it more closely resembles the seed of a darkish variety of wheat than that of common edible buckwheat. Furthermore, the flower is lighter and, most importantly, possesses the ability to self-pollinate.

The third main variety is the wild or perennial species,

Common buckwheat

Tartary buckwheat

Wild or perennial buckwheat

F. cymosum, "the probable ultimate source of both common and Tartary buckwheat, and is native to northern India and China" (Campbell). Its flower, seed shape, and style of pollination resemble common buckwheat. Yet its most commanding characteristic is that it dominates and literally takes over its surroundings. Its yellow-red root increases in size and sends out new sprouts year after year, even if the above-ground portion dies or withers during the winter. Fortunately, it is a special variety that grows only above an elevation of 10,000 feet (3,200 meters). Its leaves and roots are used as raw food and herbal teas as they contain a high degree of rutin (see Nutrition).

Since ancient times, both "original" and new strains of buckwheat have been cultivated around the world. (From here on, whenever the word "buckwheat" appears in the text, it will refer to common edible buckwheat.) Having a small whitish or pale pink flower that is an important source of nectar as well as glucoside rutin (Shevchuk, 1983), the branching and weed-like buckwheat plant, which usually grows to a height of 16 to 28 inches (40 to 71 centimeters), produces a sharp three-sided seed which turns dark brown when mature. Under the hull of the whole buckwheat grain lies a delicate light-green kernel. These kernels are commonly referred to as buckwheat groats.

Nature has wrapped buckwheat within a hard and tightly clinging hull for good reason. Once removed, buckwheat's treasured fragrance and flavor dissipate within a matter of days. In addition, the color of its hulled seed will change from a pale greenish-yellow to a rich "roasted" brown within three to four weeks. The "roasted-looking" buckwheat which you commonly find in shops is, in many cases, not roasted at all: it has changed color through long exposure to the air. Ideally, buckwheat should be turned into flour on the same day it is hulled or, at the latest, within the following three days.

In Western countries, "buckwheat hulls have very little feed value and are even detrimental as feed for pigs. Most mills burn their hulls. Some, however, sell their hulls as packing material for bottled goods and glass bulbs" (Coe). Interestingly, in Japan, the hull is used as a stuffing for pillows, something akin to the use of feathers in pillows in the West. The cool and light feeling provided by the hull has been a traditional favorite, virtually "imbedding" buckwheat in the Japanese lifestyle.

The plant itself is impressive. Its heart-shaped leaves, maroon-red stalk, clusters of white flowers, and triangular dark brown seeds have inspired more than one Oriental poet. As far back as A.D. 812 the verses of the Chinese poet Po Chu-i are recorded:

> Coming out of the gate
> And commanding the wild fields alone,
> Under the light of the shining moon,
> Buckwheat's white flowers
> Look like freshly fallen snow.

One thousand years later the following quotation was credited to a certain Miss Mitford, "Village Ser. 1 (1863)": "The beautiful buckwheat, whose transparent leaves and stalks are so brightly tinged with vermilion" (*Oxford English Dictionary*).

While a field of buckwheat does command one's

Emerging buckwheat seeds

Buckwheat flower

Maturing seeds

attention, upon close inspection it is the clusters of dainty five-petaled flowers that are most striking. Yet as attractive as these flowers are, the buckwheat plant itself has many limitations which hinder its potential for self-propagation:

If the numbers of flowers produced by a buckwheat plant is an indication of the potential seed yield of the plant, then the crop has a large unrealized yield. Studies by several investigators on possible causes of the low seed yield in relation to the number of flowers produced have focused on pollinating

THE BOOK OF SOBA

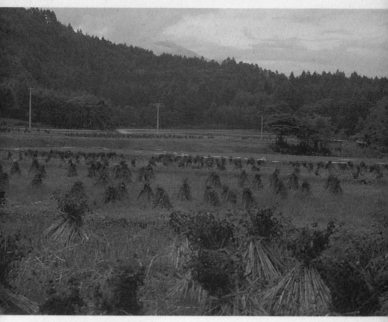

Harvested buckwheat stacked to dry

agents and on the physiology of reproduction. . . .
Free cited several studies, mostly from the U.S.S.R.,
which gave evidence that buckwheat yields can be
increased considerably by the use of honey bees.
Marshall found that under controlled conditions
buckwheat pollen can be transported by wind. In
the U.S.S.R., in the absence of bees it is apparently
customary for two persons to drag a rope with
sacks attached across the buckwheat fields, a practice which may be repeated every week or 10 days.
. . . buckwheat's low seed set is often not the
result of a lack of pollen, . . . but rather that starch

tends to accumulate in the stems of buckwheat, with a very slow rate of digestion and translocation. The translocation of starch to the developing ovaries may therefore be the limiting factor in seed-set. The spraying of growth substances on flowering plants is also reported to have resulted in a higher seed yield. (De Jong)

Since the resulting seed contains the delicate nutritional substance that will be turned into flour, and later into noodles, it is important when searching for the best quality buckwheat noodles and buckwheat flour to study what conditions will produce a superior buckwheat grain.

Moreover, if buckwheat is to yield its unique sweet fragrance and taste, it must be given specific consideration every step of the way—from the harvesting, drying, storing, and shipping stages that it goes through to reach the miller to the continued storing, milling, and shipping stages it undergoes en route to the marketplace, to the final cooking just before it is served at the dinner table.

Aside from its nutritional value, one of buckwheat's attractions as a serviceable food source lies in its ability to grow even in poor soil and in soil where neither rice nor wheat can be cultivated. Although it possesses this ability, the quality of buckwheat is nevertheless influenced by the region and soil.

What, then, are these optimum conditions? Why is it that the flour produced in Japan is sweeter and of a completely different nature than that produced in, say, the United States and Canada? Are the varieties of buckwheat structurally different, or does the final product

Buckwheat Flour

Sarashina flour

No. 1 flour

No. 2 flour

No. 3 flour

Dark flour (sanago)

Uchiko flour

Cracked groats, fine grade

Cracked groat, coarse

differ only because the methods used in taking buckwheat through all its many stages—from the fields to the millers, the millers to the soba makers or market, and from the market to the dinner table—are different? Can this difference of quality be evaluated scientifically?

A valuable hint toward answering the first question can be found by observing the areas in Japan which have long been famous for producing the highest grade of buckwheat. Just as the midwestern states of Iowa, Illinois, and Kansas are renowned as the Corn Belt of America, the areas of Nagano, Kyushu, Hokkaido, Ibaraki, and others are praised as the soba areas of Japan. It was noticed long ago that the plots located in the highland or mountain areas produced the best buckwheat. Furthermore, each is situated in an area known to register a substantial difference in temperature between day and night.

Today, it is understood that it is especially important to have cool (but not frosty) temperatures during the period when the flowers are being formed. Otherwise, good-quality buckwheat cannot be expected. For this reason, the area of Togakushi in Nagano has long been recognized as having close to perfect weather conditions for growing buckwheat. The area is often foggy, and even in the summer the temperature rarely exceeds 68°F. Although Kyushu and Hokkaido have become the leading producers of buckwheat in Japan today, the reputation of the Togakushi area for producing top-grade buckwheat still lingers in the minds of the people.

This kind of intuitive wisdom has since been supported by modern scientific research. In "Buckwheat Breeding Perspectives," agronomist Ivan Kreft states that "for efficient germination and growth of buckwheat, temperatures over 50°F are needed and those of about 68°F seem to be most effective (Sugawara, 1962; Populidi, 1976). Buckwheat is sensitive to temperatures below 34°F. Besides frosts, it is also sensitive to weather that is too warm and dry, especially during the time of flowering. When air temperatures rise above 77°F or 86°F, the flowers begin to wither. . . . Buckwheat can be grown in a variety of soils, including soils poor in nutrients and in stony fields. It is a good utilizer of insoluble phosphorus (Anderson and Thomsen, 1978). When grown in soil too rich in nitrogen, it can easily become lodged."

This leads us to the second question. What are the structural elements within buckwheat that determine its quality? Can these factors be measured scientifically?

From the viewpoint of protein content and quality, percentage of fiber, water content, and so on, no clear quantitative differences in their respective makeups could be observed. Many experts in Japan, however, are of the opinion that the makeup of the starch structure appears to vary according to the region in which buckwheat is grown. That is, the main components of amilose and amilopectine are said to be present in different ratios, according to growing area. It is this difference that is considered to be essential in creating a "real buckwheat-like" taste and texture.

Just how greatly the varieties of edible buckwheat differ from country to country is still under investigation. Yet, in addition to the inevitable differences in the soils of each country, the processing methods must also be taken into account as contributing to or diminishing the taste and fragrance of buckwheat.

Buckwheat—From Seed to Table

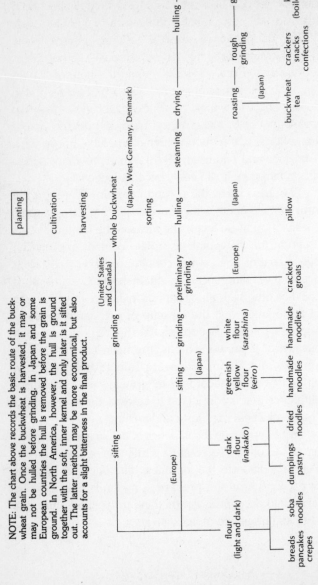

NOTE: The chart above records the basic route of the buckwheat grain. Once the buckwheat is harvested, it may or may not be hulled before grinding. In Japan and some European countries the hull is removed before the grain is ground. In North America, however, the hull is ground together with the soft, inner kernel and only later is it sifted out. The latter method may be more economical, but also accounts for a slight bitterness in the final product.

planting

cultivation

harvesting

whole buckwheat — (United States and Canada)

sorting — (Japan, West Germany, Denmark)

grinding

sifting

sifting — (Europe)

flour (light and dark)

breads
pancakes
crepes

soba noodles
noodles

grinding

sifting — (Japan)

dark flour (inakako)

dumplings
pastry
dried noodles

greenish yellow flour (seiro)

handmade noodles

white flour (sarashina)

handmade noodles

preliminary grinding — (Europe)

cracked groats

hulling — (Japan)

pillow

hulling — steaming — drying

roasting — (Japan)

buckwheat tea

rough grinding

crackers
snacks
confections

groats

kasha (boiled groats)

Buckwheat undergoes a long journey to get from the field to your table. Let's follow it as it goes from seeding to harvest, observing a few of the many Japanese proverbs about buckwheat along the way.

Buckwheat is sown soon after the danger of spring frosts has passed (in May or June) and harvested before the autumn rains and frost (in August or September). One saying goes: "Within 75 days, soba returns to the soil," meaning that soba can be harvested within that period. Another states curtly: "Soba and half-sandals are made quickly." "Half-sandals" refers to a traditional sandal used by messengers of old who, when virtually "running for a living," made use of a simple straw sandal with no heel. The saying illustrates the benefit of both of these eminently serviceable items.

About two weeks after seeding, a sprout will normally grow to 6 to 10 inches, and sometimes 12 inches, in height. Once buckwheat has sprouted, it continues to grow day and night. Ordinarily, plants stop growing at night, but buckwheat utilizes energy and nutrition stored during the day to go on growing after dark.

This is one reason that "a big difference between day and night temperatures" is a key factor to obtaining a superior quality of buckwheat. It implies that if the temperature at night becomes cool enough without freezing, buckwheat's propensity to "burn up its excess energy" will be suppressed.

After approximately one month, clusters or corollas of flowers begin to appear. Even as the flowers open, the plant continues to grow. In other words, unlike most other plant life, buckwheat's nutritional and reproductive cycles occur simultaneously.

The flowers open up and form seeds along the whole of the branch, blooming from bottom to top, continuously over a number of days. Likewise the corresponding seeds fertilize and mature at different times. After 30 days, as many as 625 flowers may be counted on a single stem. In its early stages, the seed is a beautiful dark red color. This stage has been likened to the warm glow of an old lamp: "The fire [buckwheat kernel] within the lantern [flower] is lit." As the seeds mature, they become darker still. When they reach maturity, they fall easily from their branch with only the slightest waving of the hand. This is a characteristic common among wild plants, seemingly adding credence to the opinion that the wild variety of buckwheat was the original from which the common variety evolved. Therefore, when about 70 percent of the seeds *start* to change from red to dark brown, the whole field is harvested.

After harvesting, branches of buckwheat are hung upside down tepee-style to dry in the sun for about three to seven days. This is because, as implied by the adage "It takes three days for buckwheat to realize it has been harvested," buckwheat should be treated with care, as if it is still growing. This time period allows the seed to mature, and it is said that the final product will be superior.

The buckwheat is then threshed and allowed to dry further in the wind and sun. If these two factors are sufficiently strong, good-quality buckwheat can be expected.

Recently, with advances in technology, a combine that can harvest and thresh the buckwheat in the same step has come into use. In this case, the seed is sufficiently dried with only one week of sunshine. In some cases, the buckwheat is then carried to a drying factory where a temperature-controlled wind-blowing machine is employed. Traditional millers in Japan believe that the temperatures used during the drying process should never exceed 82°F, instead of the 86°F plus often employed in America and Canada.

If less than ideal conditions are applied (say, in the event that the grain is put into a drying machine too soon), professional millers claim that they can detect a noticeable decrease in quality and freshness, which inevitably affects the taste, fragrance, and color of the buckwheat. Why this occurs is not known, but one hypothesis postulates a chemical reaction between the fat and chlorophyll in buckwheat since the kernel is still alive and growing at this stage.

Next, the harvested grain is sent to the miller's, whose task it is to turn the buckwheat into flour and groats while retaining the natural sweetness of the ripened grain.

The seed has four basic components: the outer shell (or hull), the seed coat, the endosperm tissue, and the embryo. The taste, texture, color, and fragrance exhibited by the buckwheat flour is largely determined by how the seed is ground and sifted after the outer shell is removed. That is, the buckwheat grain will yield different

A Cross Section of the Buckwheat Seed

varieties of buckwheat flour, according to the degree of sifting and, later, the ratios in which the flour from these four distinct sections are combined.

There are basically three steps in the hulling process. The first is to remove the dust, soil, and other grit that may still be clinging to the grains, and then sort the kernels according to size. The second step is to remove the hard outer shells either by steaming (for 15 minutes and then removing the hulls, producing "*kasha*") or by cracking the outer crushed hulls in a preliminary grinding process, and then removing the hulls after the milling by sifting. Although step one is easy enough to accomplish, the task of removing the outer shells completely without cracking the kernels is extremely difficult. In step three, the hulled kernels are ground together and then sifted several times. The sifting continues until most of the remaining bits of hull are removed.

In Japan, where soba noodles and other dishes have developed a strong following, the flour-making process has been honed to something resembling an art (like so much else in Japan). As such, an in-depth examination of the miller's techniques may prove invaluable not only for millers and farmers outside Japan but for discerning cooks and those concerned with nutrition.

Buckwheat that is to be ground the same day is taken out of the storage room, where it is kept at a constant 59°F (15°C), and put into a machine that will separate the buckwheat from the little twigs, sand, and other debris that inevitably accumulate during the harvesting. At the same time the hulls are cleaned and polished.

The whole buckwheat is next poured into a machine which separates the kernels according to size—large, medium, or small. This is done by a sifting machine which utilizes a series of three, progressively smaller, meshed screens.

The whole buckwheat is now put through a preliminary grinder to crack the outer protective hull: first the large-, then the medium-, and finally the small-sized kernels.

The coarsely ground grain then travels through a second type of vibrating sifter that separates grains into three basic groups: material from the seed coat, spermoderm (with a larger and smaller percentage of hulls), and the flour from the embryo/endosperm (derived from the centermost part of the buckwheat).

Although the flour from the last category is now ready for the final grinding, flour in the first two groups must pass through the preliminary stages several times. Each time a bit more of the hulls is removed. Finally, a fan-type blower is employed to separate the flour from the heavier hull material.

The cracked grain is now ready to be ground into a fine flour. There are basically two different systems for milling buckwheat: the roll method, which utilizes steel rollers, and the stone-ground method. The advantage of the former is that it is capable of producing a large quantity of flour quickly, lowering the price. Yet, since heat easily affects the quality of buckwheat, it is important not to allow the steel rollers to become too hot. The latter method is considered the ideal way of milling buckwheat because the stone grinders are carefully controlled to rotate only about 15 to 18 times per minute. In addition, the amount that enters the stone grinder with each rotation is regulated. The result is a flour which yields more viscosity during the noodle-making process, thus making it easier to obtain a successful result. However, millstones—hand-turned or electric—can grind only a fraction of what a metal-roll grinder is able to produce in the same amount of time. In olden times, the formidable weight of the heavy stone was either turned by hand or, in the case of a much larger stone, by water power. Nowadays there are electrically powered stone and roll grinding systems available that can even be used by the novice with all of the above factors basically worked out.

Although in reality it is impossible to separate and isolate each section completely, flour from the center of the grain (referred to as No. 1 flour) makes up about 25 percent, flour from the endosperm (No. 2) 35 percent, and flour from the seed coat (No. 3) 30 percent. Some factories even make a special flour, known as *uchiko*, for sprinkling on the cutting board and raw noodles to prevent sticking. The remaining 10 percent is made from that part of the buckwheat close to the shell, called No. 4 (*sanago*). The fourth grade contains a lot of the fiber and roughage and is used to make dry noodles. Some factories even produce fifth, sixth, and seventh grades. Grades 5 through 7 contain some of the outer shell and other valuable water-soluble protein, but are usually discarded, as they are difficult to work into a kneadable dough.

Interestingly enough, it is said that after World War II, geisha found a practical use for discarded No. 5 flour. At a time when not only food but other basics such as soap and cosmetics were in short supply, the geisha would wrap the flour in damp cloths and rub their skins to maintain their nice, smooth complexions. They were using the valuable water-soluble proteins which that part of buckwheat contains in such abundance.

From the specialist's point of view, the flour from the center (or endosperm tissue) of the kernel is pure white and boasts a figure of more than 1,800 B.U. of pure starch. Noting that representative varieties of wheat contain anywhere from 470 to 925 B.U., buckwheat's superiority becomes evident. It is due to the high viscosity of this starch that buckwheat noodles attain their elasticity and firmness.

After pure-white flour became available, another dimension was added to soba cuisine. Freed from the standard flour's chocolate-brown color, soba cooks began experimenting with natural coloring and flavoring agents such as fragrant citrus rind, green *shiso* leaves, black sesame seeds, red ginger, and even cherry blossoms (see Flavored Soba Noodles, page 80). This refinement appealed greatly to the aristocrats and thus the white noodles today are appropriately nicknamed *Gozen Soba*, or soba to be "served before nobles."

Although these early connoisseurs may have found the white noodles more pleasing to the palate, the part of the grain nearest the seed coat contains a considerable amount of buckwheat's protein (34 to 35 percent of the whole). Chocolate brown in color, this section contains little of the viscous starch that is present in the endosperm section, so making noodles from its flour is difficult indeed. Working to produce cohesion, however, are water-soluble proteins such as albumin and globulin. These proteins combine with water in the initial stages of mixing and produce a vitally important stickiness within the dough. Being patient enough to allow this stickiness to develop is one of the reasons why the mixing process is considered so important. In addition, wheat flour is added to ensure proper cohesiveness. Today, noodles made exclusively from this darker flour are called "country soba" (see also "Silk Cut" Soba, page 93). They are cut more thickly than regular soba noodles and are appreciated for their sweeter taste and greater chewiness.

The Future

Just as the soba chef continues to roll out the noodles and the miller strives to attain an ever-more refined buckwheat flour (with as little of the hull as possible), the breeders continue to search for a stronger and more productive strain of buckwheat.

As discussed in the History section, buckwheat does not lend itself to improvement through breeding. Even so, researchers have made some steady progress. "In 1955, the cereal crops division of the Canadian Department of Agriculture released the variety Tokyo which originally consisted of a combination of two high yielding lines selected from a Japanese introduction. The Experimental Farm at Fredericton, New Brunswick, released the Tartary buckwheat variety Welsford in 1947 for use in the Maritime provinces punctuation (McGregor)" (De Jong).

Epochal announcements were made at both Miyazaki and Shinshu universities in Japan in 1984. The agriculture departments of each of these universities succeeded virtually simultaneously in developing a buckwheat with a seed four times larger than the standard size. As their registered names Miyazaki Ootubu (Miyazaki

Large Seeds), and Shin Daigata 4-bai-tai (Shinshu University's Quadruple-sized Type) imply, they are not only bigger but of greater weight. In comparison to standard buckwheat ranging from 20 to 34 grams per 100 kernels, they weigh in at 40 to 48 grams. Moreover, the plant stem does not break easily, and so it can withstand the pressures of machine harvesting, thereby increasing yield potential. And most important, its taste is said to be every bit as good as that of original buckwheat.

Since an increase in the quantity of the harvest has also been reported, a more profitable yield seems quite possible in the future. Further, Professor Akio Ujihara announced in December 1987 the successful cross-pollination between the wild buckwheat (*F. cymosum*) from Nepal and common buckwheat (*F. esculentum*). The hope is that the new plant will be able to self-pollinate like its wild parent, and at the same time produce a seed that will cling tightly to the vine so that it can more easily be harvested, thereby increasing the overall yield.

Experiments like these provide hope, and some farmers worldwide might be persuaded to plant buckwheat in fields that have until now been almost exclusively used for rice cultivation. These new developments are also attracting great attention from scientists around the world and may eventually help to enhance world production.

Through the lineage of great botanists like Hunt, Coe, and Kellog, to modern-day specialists like Campbell, Kreft, Javornik, and others in the West, as well as Sugawara, Nagatomo, Ujihara, Adachi, and other well-respected botanists in the East, the search, study, and experimentation continues as East meets West.

Bibliography

Aihara, Cornellia. *The Do of Cooking*. Vol. 1. Oroville, Calif.: G.O.M.F. Publishing, 1972.

Aihara, Herman. *Basic Macrobiotics*. Tokyo: Japan Publications, 1985.

Aihara, Herman. *Macrobiotics: A Key to Happiness*. Oroville, Calif.: G.O.M.F. Publishing, 1977.

Campbell, C. G. "Buckwheat Fagopyrum (Polygonaceae)." In *Evolution of Crop Plants*. Ed. N. W. Simmonds. London and New York: Longman, 1976.

Coe, Maynard R. "Buckwheat Milling and Its By-Products." U. S. Department of Agriculture Circular no. 190. Washington: December 1931.

De Candolle, Alphonse. *The Origins of Cultivated Plants*. 1881. Reprinted as part of the International Scientific Series. New York: D. Appleton and Company, 1908.

De Jong, H. "Buckwheat." *Field Crop Abstracts* 25 no. 3 (August 1972).

Eggum, Bjorn O. "The Protein Quality of Buckwheat in Comparison with Other Protein Sources of Plant or Animal Origin." In *Buckwheat Research 1980: Proceedings of the 1st International Symposium on Buckwheat*. Ljubljana, Yugoslavia: Organizing Committee of the 1st International Symposium on Buckwheat, 1980.

Eggum, Bjorn O., Ivan Kreft, and Branka Javornik. "Chemical composition and protein quality of buckwheat (Fagopyrum esculentum moench)." Netherlands: Martinus Nijhoff/Dr. W. Junk, 1981.

Everett, Thomas H., ed. *The New York Botanical Garden Illustrated Encyclopedia of Horticulture*. Vol 4. New York and London: Garland Publishing, 1981.

Fujimura, Masao. *Soba no gijutsu* (Soba technique). Tokyo: Shokuhin Shuppansha, 1980.

Furuzawa, Norio. *Iwate no soba* (Soba of Iwate Prefecture). Morioka Japan: Kumagai Insatsu, 1985.

Great Soviet Encyclopedia: A Translation of the Third Edition. Vol. 7. New York: Macmillan; London: Collier Macmillan, 1972.

Hagami, Rev. Shocho. "Mt. Hiei and Buckwheat." In *Buckwheat Research 1983: Proceedings of the 2nd International Symposium on Buckwheat*. Ed. Takashi Nagamoto and Taiji Adachi. Miyazaki, Japan: Organizing Committee of the 2nd International Symposium on Buckwheat, 1983.

Harlan, Jack R. "Agricultural Origins: Centers and Noncenters." *Science* 174 (October 1971).

Hunt, Thomas F. *The Cereals in America*. New York: Orange Judd Company; London: Kegan Paul, Trench, Trubner and Co., Ltd., 1914.

International Symposium on Buckwheat, Ljubljana, Yugoslavia, 1980. *Buckwheat Research 1980: Proceedings of the 1st International Symposium on Buckwheat*. Ljubljana, Yugoslavia: Organizing Committee of the 1st International Symposium on Buckwheat, 1980. See also under Eggum, Bjorn O.; Javornik,

Branka, and Ivan Kreft; and Kreft, Ivan, and Branka Javornik.

International Symposium on Buckwheat, Miyazaki, Japan, 1983. *Buckwheat Research 1983: Proceedings of the 2nd International Symposium on Buckwheat*. Miyazaki, Japan: Organizing Committee of the 2nd International Symposium on Buckwheat, 1983. See also under Hagami, Rev. Shocho; Kreft, Ivan; and Javornik, Branka.

Japan Science and Technology Agency. *Standard Tables of Food Composition in Japan*. 4th ed. Tokyo: 1982.

Javornik, Branka. "Nutritional Quality and Composition of Buckwheat Proteins." In *Buckwheat Research 1983: Proceedings of the 2nd International Symposium on Buckwheat*. Ed. Takashi Nagamoto and Taiji Adachi. Miyazaki, Japan: Organizing Committee of the 2nd International Symposium on Buckwheat, 1983.

Javornik, Branka, and Ivan Kreft. "The Structure of the Buckwheat Kernel." In *Buckwheat Research 1980: Proceedings of the 1st International Symposium on Buckwheat*. Ljubljana, Yugoslavia: Organizing Committee of the 1st International Symposium on Buckwheat, 1980.

Kaneko, Manpei. *Shinshu soba no hanashi* (Shinshu soba wisdom). 1975. Reprint Japan: Shinshu Ginga Shobo, 1979.

Kreft, Ivan. "Buckwheat Breeding Perspectives." In *Buckwheat Research 1983: Proceedings of the 2nd International Symposium on Buckwheat*. Ed. Takashi Nagamoto and Taiji Adachi. Miyazaki, Japan: Organizing Committee of the 2nd International Symposium on Buckwheat, 1983.

Kreft, Ivan, and Branka Javornik. "Traditional Processing and Utilization of Buckwheat in Yugoslavia." In *Buckwheat Research 1980: Proceedings of the 1st International Symposium on Buckwheat*. Ljubljana, Yugoslavia: Organizing Committee of the 1st International Symposium on Buckwheat, 1980.

Muramoto, Noboru. *Healing Ourselves*. Avon, N.Y.: Avon Press, 1972.

Nasu, Keisuke. *Kenko soba* (Healthful soba). Tokyo: Nosan Gyoson Bunka Kyokai, 1984.

Niijima, Shigeru. *Soba nyumon* (An introduction to soba). Tokyo: Hoiku-sha, 1975.

Niijima, Shigeru, and Shigehisa Shibata. *Menrui hyakka jiten* (Encyclopedia of noodles). Tokyo: Shokuhin Shuppan-sha, 1984.

Nishio, Yoshihiro. "Hinoemata no soba ryori" (Soba cooking of Hinoemata [home of the "silk cut" soba]). In *Tohoku II*, Vol. 2 of *Nihon no kyodo ryori* (Japanese country cooking). Tokyo: Gyosei, 1986.

Ohsawa, George. *The Philosophy of Oriental Medicine*. Vol. 2, *The Book of Judgment*. 1960. 2d ed. published as *The Book of Judgment*. New York: Ohsawa Foundation, 1966.

———. *Zen Cookery: The Philosophy of Oriental Culture*. Vol. 1, *Practical Macrobiotics*. 1963. Reprint. Los Angeles: Ignoramus Press, 1966.

Oxford English Dictionary—New English Dictionary on Historical Principles. London: Oxford, 1933.

Sekai Bunka Sha. *Furusato soba udon* (Country-style soba and udon). Tokyo, 1984.

———. *Soba*. In *Oishii men* (Delicious noodles). Tokyo, 1983.

Sherry, Robert W. *Plants for Man*. 2d ed. Englewood Cliffs, N.J.: Prentice-Hall Inc., 1972.

Shibata Shoten. *Masshiro ni saita soba: soba mukashi banashi* (The white blossoming soba: Tales of soba). Tokyo, 1984.

——. *Soba udon gijutsu kyohon* (A manual of soba and udon technique). Vol. 1, *Soba no kihon gijutsu* (Basic soba technique). Tokyo, 1983. Vol. 2, *Soba udon no oyo gijutsu* (Advanced techniques of soba and udon). Tokyo, 1985.

——. *Soba udon: New Menu*. Tokyo, 1986.

Shurtleff, William, and Akiko Aoyagi. *The Book of Tofu*. 1973. Reprint. Berkeley: Ten Speed Press, 1983.

Takase, Reibun. *Soba no hon* (The book of soba). Tokyo: Bunka Shuppan Kyoku, 1983.

Tsuchiya, Yoshio. *A Feast for the Eyes: The Japanese Art of Food Arrangement*. Tokyo and New York: Kodansha International, 1985.

Tsuji, Keisuke. *Shitekiso shoku no kenko ho* (The healthy way of balanced eating). Tokyo: Kobunsha, 1983.

——. "Soba no eiyo" (The multi-working nutritional power of buckwheat). *Soba udon* 14 (June 1984).

Tsuji, Shizuo. *Japanese Cooking: A Simple Art*. Tokyo and New York: Kodansha International, 1980.

Tsuji, Shizuo, and Koichiro Hata. *Practical Japanese Cooking: Easy and Elegant*. Tokyo and New York: Kodansha International, 1986.

Uehara, Jiro, and Ryuichi Satsuma. *Soba no hon* (The book of soba). Tokyo: Shibata Shoten, 1969.

Uji, Masami. "Soba yo sake yo te o tsunage" (Soba and saké join hands). In *Soba shikomi-cho sekenbanashi* (Soba preparation and discussion). Nagano, Japan: Ginga Shobo, 1987.

Ujihara, Akio. *Soba no kagaku: Nihon soba no ruutsu to soba no shokumotsubutsu* (The roots and history of buckwheat as a foodstuff). Tokyo: Mainichi Shinbunsha Shuppan, 1981.

——. "Studies on the ecological features and the potentials as breeding materials of Asian common buckwheat varieties (Fagopyrum esculentum M.)." Tokyo: Ministry of Education and Ministry of Agriculture, Forestry and Fisheries, 1983.

Vaviloff, N. I. *The Origin, Variation, Immunity and Breeding of Cultivated Plants* (in Russian). 1934. Translated by K. Starr Chester in *Selected Writings of N. I. Vavilov*. Waltham, Mass.: Chronica Botanica, 1950.

Yoneda, Soei. *The Heart of Zen Cuisine*. Originally published as *Good Food from a Japanese Temple*. 1982. Tokyo and New York: Kodansha International, 1987.

Index

Acknowledgments

I wish to express my gratitude to all those who have given me support, assistance, and advice on this project and over the years:

To my three soba teachers, Takao Abe of Take Yabu, Shigeru Fujimori of Fujisei, and Ikuma Yamamoto of Honjinbo for allowing me to work and train within the confines of their traditional shops, thereby giving me the chance to study the art backstage. Their perseverance and pride inspired me to take the job seriously.

To the soba masters of Honmura-an, Wakatake, Shungetsu, and Okina for welcoming me into their establishments and teaching me the secrets of home milling, emphasizing that quality home grinding can be done successfully. To Yoshiyuki Oyama of Honjinbo and Fumio Hirai of Take Yabu for their assistance in preparing the menu for the color photographs. To Tae Moriyama, Tami Ejima, Hideo Sakai, Chiyako Hatsuyama, Chika Furukawa, and many others whose help was indispensable in helping me meet the formidable challenge of reading vital Japanese texts.

To William and Akiko Shurtleff, who, in addition to providing a wealth of specific research contributions which added immeasurable depth to my own understanding of soba and its history in the West, have been trusty consultants on how to introduce soba to the West. To Yuuchihi Nagata for providing me with a variety of written material on soba in Japanese and for kindly introducing me to the soba historian Shigeru Niijima, and Professor and Mrs. Akio Ujihara of Shinshu University. Hosting me on three separate occasions, Ujihara's broad knowledge and understanding of soba greatly enlarged my own vision. To Yachiyo ("As in the Japanese national anthem") and Yoshinaka Hirano of the "Corner store" (Kadoya) in Hinoemata, Fukushima Prefecture, for their kindness and assistance in the teaching and demonstration of the "Silk Cut" method and other country originals, and to Morikatsu Hiran for demonstrating the traditional *kibachi*-making method. To Satsuma Uichi, president of the highly respected Mimi-yu restaurant, for showing me the workings of his restaurant in Kyobashi, where, in addition to maintaining a unique expertise in udon noodle making, they take pride in creating fine soba. To Dr. Bjorn Eggum and Professor Ivan Kreft for supplying important scientific data in time to reach the publication deadline, and to Dr. Keisuke Tsuji, who spent three afternoons making sure I understood his nutrition report, as well as correcting mistakes in the final draft.

To my brothers Drs. Robert and Richard Udesky, for their encouragement in the promotion of a food that is "low in fat and cholesterol free." To my sister, Joan, who knew from the start that I was up to something more than just making noodles and has been faithfully keeping me up-to-date on developments in the Natural Food movement back home. To the friends and colleagues who, over the last fifteen years, have helped me, directly and indirectly, in the writing of this book: Mark Gray who was with me throughout the eight years of training and writing in Japan; Bob and Martha Newmiller; Elliott Lash; Jacob Israel; and Dr. Richard Harris, who introduced me to the way of Natural Food in America. To Noboru Muramoto, and Herman and Cornellia Aihara for initially sending me to Japan in 1977, and whose guidance and fundamental teachings from 1972 to 1976 continue to serve me tremendously.

To Ryuji Koseta of the Federation of Japan Noodle Organizations, representing more than 20,000 soba shops in Japan, for his untiring assistance and dedication to the promotion of soba. Special thanks go to Hitoshi Matsuura of the Japan Victor Company and Shigeo Sugawa and Tatsu Yasuhara of Dentsu for their encouragement, guidance, and unselfish support, spurring me on until the end. To Kenzaburo Mogi and Linda Sakamoto of the Kikkoman Corporation for their generosity and interest in this project. To Yasuo and Koji Ishimori of the Ishimori Buckwheat Milling Company for extending their cooperation and hospitality on many occasions. To Peter Dowling for his assistance in preparing this pocket-sized edition.

Finally, thanks are in order to the people at Kodansha International: Koki Mori for his expert counsel; Barry Lancet for his fine editing and for first suggesting I bring my manuscript to KI; Makiko Sasaki for her editorial work; Shigeo Katakura for his design; Kensuke Tada, Prue Moodie, and Michiko Tsukamoto for help in the final hour; and lastly, to Keiji Suzuki, whose love of soba rivals my own, and whose encouragement continues to give me hope that buckwheat will finally receive its due attention in the West, and once again demonstrate its true status as a food of the people.